Act As If
Stumbling through Hollywood with Headshot in Hand

Copyright ©2014 Petrea Burchard

All rights reserved.

Published by
Boz Books
BozBooks.net

Book design by Paula L. Johnson
Author photo by Skye Moorhead

ISBN 985883758
ISBN 13 978-0-9858837-5-1

Also by Petrea Burchard
Camelot & Vine

This book is dedicated to
actors everywhere.

Screw the odds.

jour-ney-man [jur-nee-muhn]

n., pl. -men.
1. a reliable but unremarkable worker or performer.
2. a person hired to do work for another, usually by the day.
3. a person who has an apprenticeship at a trade and is certified to work at it under another person.

TABLE OF CONTENTS

Foreword xi
Introduction..xiii
1. Career Woman 1
2. Screw the Odds 5
3. Connections... 9
4. Flashy Fish... 13
5. Order vs Chaos.. 17
6. A Boy and His Face... 21
7. The Green-Eyed Monster 25
8. Test 29
9. Desperation Stinks 31
10. Ready.. 35
11. My Instrument 41
12. Excuses 45
13. Primal Scene.. 49
14. An Ensemble Crew 53
15. My Feel-Good Audition Song 57
16. Inner Bohemian 61
17. Glad to Be Here 65

18. Drop Everything 69
19. Nor Ham Nor Bacon 73
20. You Persevere 77
21. Lethargy 81
22. Relentlessly Loopy 85
23. Saying It Forward 89
24. Novocain 93
25. So, That Happened 97
26. Do-Over 101
27. Pro Choice 105
28. Ryoko Rocks 109
29. Blessing-Counting Time 113
30. 'Tis the Season 117
31. Ageism 119
32. I AM the Hot Flash! 123
33. My Lucky Break 127
34. How I Spent My Summer Vacation 131
35. Channel Surfing 135
36. The Kindest Cut 139
37. En Garde! 145
38. Pollyanna's Lament 149
39. Still Hoping 153
40. Interesting Lives, Part One 157
41. Interesting Lives, Part Two 161
42. Interesting Lives, Part Three 165
43. Yes/And 169
Acknowledgments 173
About the Author 175

FOREWORD

On July 21, 2004, Petrea Burchard's first article appeared in *Actors Ink*. It was titled "Flashy Fish." In it she said, "Hollywood is full of the prettiest, smartest, funniest and most talented people from every graduating class in every high school in every home town. It's one huge pond and all the fish are flashy." From there she went on to create a darkly funny list of ways to make it in Hollywood, thus beginning a wonderful streak of 100 articles, all of them finely written with Petrea's wry, dry, dark humor balanced by a penetrating look at the truth of what it means to be an actor in Hollywood.

The more she wrote, the more she revealed about herself, thus revealing the poet inside her. I would suggest flipping to her story, "Interesting Lives" (Parts One, Two and Three). As Petrea writes about a dream come true, she allows us a peek into a deeper and more important truth: the need to discover who we are, because sometimes our dreams can lock us into shallow lives. Within these three very short articles she also presents us with two gorgeous images/ideas:

Time melts like a candle
Dreams aren't actions

And this is just the tip of the iceberg of what awaits you. With each piece of writing, Petrea conjures up a gem of insight. To experience how deep Petrea's skill as a writer grew as she continued to send me article after article, read "Primal Scene."

It was a wonderful time for me, to receive 100 new articles from Petrea, each fresh off of her word processor, each pulling me deeper into wanting to know: what comes next?

Richard Gilbert-Hill
Editor
Actors Ink eMag

INTRODUCTION

When I arrived in Hollywood I knew two people.

My friend, a writer and stand-up comic, invited me to stay at her home in Burbank for a couple of weeks while she helped me find an apartment. The other person I knew, her husband, helped me get the essential day job so I wasn't desperate for acting work to pay the bills. I was grateful for their support at a time when I was so scared I kept having to pull over and park to hyperventilate.

And I was hopeful. So hopeful. I was a walking quivering lip.

Arriving in Hollywood with a million dreams in your suitcase and zero connections in your address book is terrifying. You can be the biggest fish from your hometown pond, but you're in the ocean now.

When you show up at your first audition and most auditions thereafter, you've still got all that hope and fear. But you can't let your lip quiver or you won't get the job (unless your character is supposed to be scared, then use it!). It's entirely possible, even probable, that you won't get the job anyway, but fear turns that probability into a sure thing.

So you act as if.

Acting as if is pretending or believing something is true until it becomes true. This is not like using brain waves to lose weight, get dates or fly. Let's face it, those things take actual diligence. But acting as if does work on your brain when your attitude needs a new direction. Some things you have control over, some you don't. You control your perception, and your perception is all.

You act as if you're not scared. You act as if you know you're right for the part, even though you're forty and the character description says fifteen. You act as if you didn't just drive an hour to get to the audition and you didn't search for parking for an additional twenty minutes and your armpits don't stink like you've been hauling hay bales all day in the burning sun. Because really, you're the only person who knows.

When act as if becomes reality, you've shaken off all that. You aren't scared anymore. You are right for the part. You're still forty, but a young-looking forty. Your armpits may stink, but the character's do, too. You have confidence, you have power, and your audition is great.

You don't have to be an actor to act as if. This technique is useful in all sorts of situations. You can act as if:

    ... you understand what your date just said, though you're dying to ask, "What does 'erudite' mean?";

    ... you enjoyed the show, and your friend's performance had the mark of genius;

    ... you're qualified in Linux even if you don't have the faintest idea how to code;

    ... you're not dying for that person to call you;

… you're enjoying the sex;
… the food doesn't suck;
… you like jazz.

You can act as if your car didn't break down yesterday, or your girlfriend didn't just dump you, or you didn't just return from a loved one's funeral—though if that's the case for heaven's sake, you're allowed to book out for a few days. The audition is, after all, a business situation, and not an opportunity to tell the casting director your problems.

I also recommend you don't confide those problems to the other actors in the waiting room. ("I have to get this job. My husband left me and the debt is all in my name!" "I was just in an accident and I limped a mile to get here!") Most actors will be supportive, but there's one, just one, who would love to go into the Casting Director's office and tell her what a basket case you are.

And by the way, don't be the person who does that. Don't pick on other actors, ever. Once, while waiting to audition, I looked up to see the actor who'd auditioned before me as she came out of the room. We were in a play together at the time and I was glad to see her. When I opened my mouth to say hi, she saw me, pointed at my hair and said, "Love the fake blonde!" loud enough for the casting director and everyone in the waiting room to hear.

Not that she was wrong. But neither of us got the part. I was too rattled and she was too bitchy. Casting Directors don't want to work with you if you're easily rattled, and especially not if you're bitchy.

It would have been superb if I'd walked into the audition room and made a joke. "She's such a kidder. My natural color is blue, but I wasn't getting work so I thought I'd try blonde."

That might have relaxed us all. But this took place before I knew how to act as if. Instead of taking the opportunity for a good quip, I walked into an awkward situation with a casting director who felt embarrassed for me. I would have had a better chance at the part if she'd hated me. And I couldn't concentrate on my audition because I was already planning my revenge.

Which I got, years later, though my kidding frenemy will never know. Acting as if you live well can be uplifting. And pretty soon, hallelujah, it's the best revenge.

In *Act As If,* I offer a selection of essays from my column that appeared in the *ActorsInk* eMagazine of NowCasting.com. These stories are about the times I did, and did not, act as if while working in Hollywood. Sometimes I didn't need to. And sometimes, boy, did I ever.

But more often than not we know what we're doing. All we have to do is be ourselves.

Petrea Burchard

Act As If
Stumbling through Hollywood with Headshot in Hand

Petrea Burchard

Boz Books

CHAPTER 1
CAREER WOMAN

I carry a sleek, leather briefcase. I'm dressed in a severe, all-business power suit. The skirt is a conservative yet attractive length. The heels of my shoes are just high enough to be painful. The shoes match my suit. Navy blue.

I approach the desk. I check my watch. I'm agitated. An underling is late. I sit at the desk and, with manicured nails, type something on the computer keyboard—something important.

I'm the boss.

I wear a giant basketball on my head.

Who am I and what am I doing?

Right. I'm an actor, auditioning for a commercial.

One of my favorite things about commercial auditions is that the process is impossible to explain to the uninitiated. Each experience is unique. Yesterday I danced in the arms of a strange man in an imaginary kitchen. The day before, I mimed a menu and read from it, ordering filet mignon and gratefully accepting an empty plate from a charming waiter. Last week I sat in an airport lounge with a harmonica holder around my neck. Instead of a harmonica, a mangled hamburger bun was poised before my lips. I pretended to eat it, but I didn't dare take a bite because that bun had been working all day. I got a callback for that one, so I got two chances to savor that lipstick-covered ick.

I look forward to seeing that spot.

Sometimes I even book the job, but the ratio of bookings to auditions doesn't explain why I pursue the bizarre profession of commercial acting. I don't do it for art, although there's definitely skill involved. Nor do I do it for money, really. The occasional commercial pays well, but if I were looking for financial security I'd be producing commercials, not acting in them.

Nope. I do it because it suits me. I've worked in a real office. I got bored fast. I've worked in actual stores and found retail to be dull. I've waited tables and served plates of real food. It was absolute drudgery. All jobs I've tried besides acting have had one thing in common: they were bland.

Pursuing commercial work may be difficult but even on days when it's awful, it's never dull. I've been a parent to a seven-year-old with a résumé twice as impressive as mine. I've rowed a boat, smiled too broadly, screamed at the top of my lungs, enjoyed a picnic on the sand, ridden a flying trapeze, sold everything from toothpaste to real estate, mimed everything from a swing-set to a stallion, piloted a passenger jet, ridden in a hot-air balloon and sailed the seven seas, all in audition rooms with the featureless appeal of a drunk-tank.

I continue to slog through the traffic, lug several changes of clothes and even suffer the occasional indignity because I don't want the routine of a day job. Yes, it would be nice to have a regular paycheck. But to get it I'd have to trade my erratic schedule for a tomorrow that's very much like today. To me, that kind of certainty is scary.

I'm fortunate because my working life is as I want it to be: unpredictable. I hope I can keep it up, otherwise I'll have to wear those excruciating shoes and that business suit for real, without the added perk of a basketball on my head.

CHAPTER 2

SCREW THE ODDS

When I moved to Los Angeles to seek acting success, I didn't know the odds were against me. I didn't know that a brand new kid in town couldn't book a juicy co-star role on a prime-time drama. So I booked one.

— THE END —

It's a nice little story. But you already know there's more.

Immediately, people told me how unusual it was for someone like me to get a job like that. Over coffee with friends, the conversation included such encouraging phrases as "the odds are against you," and "that job was a fluke."

My agent at the time said I was "not well connected," which tells us something about his own self-image. He went on to warn me that it was going to be tough to get me auditions, let alone actual paying work. I was thirty-three years old and "no spring chicken."

(Now that I'm beyond thirty-three—hell, now that I'm beyond *forty-three*, I know what a spring chicken is and is not. But I digress.)

I began to believe the naysayers. To my mind, the actors I was competing with were more famous, better connected, skinnier and more beautiful than I was. Every time I auditioned I felt like I was up against Meryl Streep.

I'm a big fan of Ms. Streep but I wasn't a big fan of myself, and once I knew the odds were against me every meeting or audition was a chance to prove it. Rather than approaching an opportunity with the attitude of "I'm going to show them what I can do," I went in with the certainty that everyone else who auditioned would do better.

This can't help but become a self-fulfilling prophecy. I don't care what you do to mask your attitude. Go to an audition with a toothy smile on your face and pretend all the confidence you want, but if you believe the odds are against you, look around: you'll see the casting directors plugging their noses. The stench of low self-esteem is upon you.

Soon I wasn't working or even auditioning. My agent, the guy who thought so little of himself, thought even less of me and dropped me. I joined a theater company where I paid dues, built sets, cleaned toilets, worked the box office and paid more dues. I was rarely cast in the plays, and when I was, I got only small parts.

At my day job at a commercial production company, the post-production supervisor thought I had a good voice. She hired me to do some in-house voice-overs. It was fun, and I learned on the job. I could stop by the studio, record on my lunch hour, and even make a few bucks. After several small successes I got the idea to try working in radio. I didn't know much about it but I asked some pros for help, put together a demo and sent it out. I got a job as an overnight weekend D.J. at a small station an hour north of Los Angeles, and within a few months I was doing traffic reports on afternoon drive in L.A.

A friend said to me, "Do you know the odds of that happening? Do you know how hard it is to get work in L.A. radio?"

"Nope," I said, "and I don't want to know."

— THE END —

CHAPTER 3

CONNECTIONS

Hollywood is all about connections. "It's not what you know, it's who you know," they say.

Doesn't that piss you off? Why does my career have to be about who I schmooze? How many powerful behinds do I have to kiss to be an actor? And how is that art?

My friend Blanche and I used to complain about the connections thing. We moved to L.A. from Chicago at about the same time. She was "hip-pocketed" by a power agency, which meant they sent her on auditions but didn't sign her to a contract, though they pocketed 10% of what she made. I signed with a smaller organization—the kind with a funky upstairs office in Hollywood where there's only one guy running the place, so if any calls come in during lunch they aren't answered because the guy's too cheap to get voice mail—in other words, "a boutique agency with a select client list."

Blanche and I both auditioned for everything we could

get our hands on, which wasn't much because we weren't well connected. Between day jobs we hung out, drank coffee, shared secrets, commiserated about the Hollywood ass-kissing conundrum and became good friends.

I eventually got a better agent, or at least a better agency. Okay, they had a better office. They didn't call me very often. In fact they were never excited about me. But I filled a "hole" in their roster. Kind of like spackle in rotted wood.

Blanche and I produced a showcase together. She starred in a play and I understudied for her in a pinch. She came to see me in a few awful basement productions and told me I was great. She got married and had a kid. I babysat so much I became "Auntie Petrea" to her little one. And when I married my Mr. Right, Blanche and her husband performed the ceremony. They even dog-sit Phiz, and he's a chewer.

Obviously, Blanche and I are close. She's my beloved friend.

Who knew she would one day decide to quit acting and open a talent agency?

It wouldn't be easy. No one had heard of the new agency. It would be tough to get producers and casting directors to open Blanche's submission envelopes, tougher still to get her calls returned. When she asked me to be one of the first actors to sign with her, I had a difficult choice to make. Should I go with a new, unknown agent who scrambles to submit me because she loves me and believes in my talent? Or should I stay with a well-known agency with a nice office where I could be…spackle?

Hmm.

I stuck with my friend because I believed in her as much as she believed in me. I knew she could break down the barriers and have a successful agency, just as she knew I could book paying work when given the opportunity to audition for roles that were right for me. It took time, but we've done it. I've finally got a reputable agent who actually pitches me, as opposed to an underpaid assistant who sticks a post-it on my photo and sends it off, hoping it'll land somewhere near a studio. And Blanche has a client who is eternally grateful, helps in the office, and will never consider going with another agent unless or until Blanche retires.

I finally get it—the thing about connections—and I've stopped complaining about it. A connection is not a person you schmooze. It's not a butt you kiss. It's someone who knows you, cares about you, trusts you and wants to work with you. That takes a lot more than lunch at the Four Seasons. If Blanche's agency were to close tomorrow or if I were to switch careers and become a matador, Blanche and I would still be friends. That's what connects us.

I'm not suggesting you stop complaining about connections. I'm suggesting you look across the top of your coffee cup and notice who you're complaining to. Maybe one day that person will be your big connection. Better yet, *you* might be the big shot. If you produced a big-budget movie and got to work with whomever you chose, wouldn't you hire people you trust, people you like, people you can stand to talk to all day? I would.

If Blanche needed her ass kissed, she knows I'd kiss it for her because she busted it for me. But I know she'd never ask me.

That's what I call a connection.

CHAPTER 4
FLASHY FISH

Every actor who moves to the big city to give it a shot was once a big fish in a small pond. It's so true it's cliché. We won the acting competitions, received a lot of attention and got good grades. Or at least we were voted class clown.

It was great while it lasted, wasn't it? Then we came to Hollywood and everything changed. Nobody paid attention to us anymore and we became just another headshot.

Hollywood is full of the prettiest, smartest, funniest and most talented people from every graduating class in every high school in every hometown. It's one huge pond and all the fish are flashy. You're no longer the most talented. Everyone's talented. You're no longer the most beautiful. Everyone's beautiful, or at least funny. Now that you're here, how are you going to stand out?

While things are slow in the summer it's a good time to revive your career by trying something new. Here are a few suggestions:

1. ***Send cute presents to all the casting directors.***
    This has been done, but if you come up with something unique it might be worth a shot. Let me know if you do.

    No matter how I try, I can't come up with anything new. Pencils inscribed with the phrase, "Hire Me!," cookies frosted with your contact information, harmonicas that come with two free airline tickets to Paris and sing your name like a chorus of angels when they're played—all have been done, done, done. You might try a bottle of wine but not everyone wants alcohol (and some who want it shouldn't have it). Or you could personalize a giant chocolate bar with your headshot.

    Whatever you do, don't use too many exclamation points! It's too cute!!! They'll think you're trying too hard!!!!!!!!

2. ***Skip the middleman and go to the top: write directly to the producers.***
    Just remember to keep your letter short because (I've heard) their lips get tired.

3. ***Streak through the studio backlots.***
    Do this only if you're absolutely certain that the sight of you naked will not be a detriment to your career.

4. ***Try pornography.***
    The success rate is low, but there was one crossover star, once. You could be next.

5. ***Hire a plane and sky-write your name and phone number above Sunset Boulevard.***
    Frankly, I don't recommend this. Nobody looks up, they're too absorbed in the schmooze. Plus the crank calls get too personal. It would be better to:

6. Take someone powerful to lunch.
I used to love doing this but I maxed out my credit cards. And I'm always getting something splashed on my shirt or stuck in my teeth.

7. Get your picture up on some billboards.
It may not get you any work but it will make you famous, which is great if you don't care what you get famous for.

8. Plaster your name and headshot all over your beat-up sedan.
I don't know…does that work?

9. Sleep with producers.
This is a time-honored Hollywood tradition. I've heard it's a road to success. I even had a manager once tell me that the only way to make it in the business was to become proficient at oral sex. Hooray!!!! Anyone can do that!!!!!! (I haven't tried it because, well, see item 6.) There's no guarantee of a role but you might at least get a beer. And don't put this one off. After about age 23 you're no longer a spring chicken. Producers prefer to have their sex with spring chickens. And don't forget item 2.

10. Be professional and do good work.
Never mind. That one's been done to death.

CHAPTER 5
ORDER VS CHAOS

I'm one of those people you might call "anal." It's an unattractive term for an orderly person who is, mind you, not necessarily unattractive. I'm not obsessive-compulsive to the point of exhibiting the so-named disorder, but you could call me an OCD sympathizer. I like having everything in place. I alphabetize my books and organize them on the shelves by category. I balance my checkbook every day. And—okay, I admit it—I fold my undies.

At least I don't iron them.

How could someone like me be an artist?

I used to think I was an impostor. I thought actors had to be wild and out of control. They had to be poor. They had to drink and smoke and wear baggy clothes from resale shops, and have sex with the wrong people.

All of that was fun for a while, but it wasn't me. Maybe I wasn't destined to be an actor.

Then I discovered the 19th century French novelist and

playwright Gustave Flaubert, who made me think maybe I really do have an artistic temperament. Flaubert said, "Be regular and orderly in your life, so that you may be violent and original in your work."

Every time I read that I feel vindicated. If I apply it to my folded underwear I begin to think maybe I *should* iron it.

But Flaubert was only partly right. Along with the violence and originality in your work, you need order in there, too.

Way back in Acting 101, our teacher showed us how to perform a monologue. He launched into a speech that involved crying real tears, screaming, and self-flagellation. It was emotional. It was real. It was painful.

I mean it was painful for the audience. He was crying so hard we couldn't understand a word he said. He had all the violence and originality, but there wasn't any order in there. That's what technique is for, and we walk a fine line between that and our emotions. Sometimes we need to get down deep and feel what needs feeling, but we also have to make sure we say our lines, hit our marks, face the audience or the camera, and make ourselves understood. It doesn't matter if you're in the moment if the audience isn't in there with you.

Order *and* chaos.

Yesterday, a friend and I walked in a beautiful garden. Trees and flowers grew along shaded pathways that twisted amid the underbrush. I said, "I think we like the shapes of nature because they're unpredictable and asymmetrical." My friend answered, "Yes, but in this garden some plants are wild, others are pruned. There are paths, and there are hidden places. There's enough violence here to intrigue us, and enough order to make us feel safe."

The chaos of art intrigues us with its asymmetry. The order of our technique makes us comfortable enough to allow the violence to show.

I don't want to know how that applies to my underpants.

CHAPTER 6

A BOY AND HIS FACE

"She had to pick the locks herself, but other than that, the new boyfriend's a keeper," said Roxy, snapping her menu open.

"Outstanding," I said, opening mine.

"Can we get some service over here?" The guy at the next table sounded irritated.

"I'll be right back." Our adorable waiter dashed off to grab more menus. He'd been as wrapped up in Roxy's tale as I had.

Roxy knows how to tell a story. She's been writing and producing television sitcoms for almost 15 years. We try not to talk business when we get together, but we always find our way to the subject because there's so much to talk about, and Roxy's got the poop. She's written and produced her own show as well as someone else's, and was co-executive producer of more than 100 episodes of a hit sitcom that ran for ages and made stars out of its entire cast.

So when Roxy talks business, I listen. After Adorable

Waiter brought our lunch, Roxy told me the story of her friend Charlie.

"I've known Charlie since he was in his mother's womb," she said. "When he came to L.A. to be an actor, he asked my advice on how to start."

"Good move," I said.

Charlie didn't have formal acting training, Roxy told me. He knew how to improvise and that was about it. That and three bucks will get you a cup of coffee in L.A. Roxy told me she thought carefully about her advice before giving it. Knowing the business, and having known Charlie all his life, she thought he should take advantage of his most unique characteristic: his face.

"Nobody has a face like Charlie's," she said. "He's got a funny face. He wanted to get head shots with all kinds of costumes and looks. I told him not to bother. All he needed was a close-up of his face. No smiling or frowning, just those big, wide eyes. His 'Charlie' face."

Charlie took Roxy's advice. He brought her his proof sheets and she chose the Charliest photo in the bunch. He sent it out, got a commercial agent and was soon called in for his first audition.

Charlie, as we know by now, was no dummy. He called Roxy and asked her advice again. He wasn't sure what the casting director would want and he had those improv skills…

"I told him, 'You will *never* know what they want.' He was going to audition with an accent!" Roxy waved her napkin like a white flag. "I said, 'Don't you dare. You walk in there and look at that camera and just say your line. That is all. Don't do anything else. Just be Charlie. If they ask you to improvise, go ahead, but not before.'"

My quiche quivered at the end of my fork. I was riveted. Aren't talent and training important, I wondered? "Did he do it?"

"He did it and he booked the job."

"Wow!" I said.

"Damn!" said the potted plant next to our table. It sounded a lot like Adorable Waiter.

"Check, please," said the guy at the next table.

Roxy had more to say about acting and auditions, but I was intrigued by the story of Charlie and his face. You may not like it, especially if you've spent your savings on classical training and on-camera workshops. (Or facelifts, Botox and veneers.) Maybe Charlie will spend some of his vast earnings (from six national commercials so far) on acting classes, but you could argue he doesn't need to. "All he has to do is look at the camera!" says Roxy.

I had a lot to ponder. Anybody can take classes. Anybody can become trained. And you should, because training always comes in handy. When you choose to make your living as an actor, you're joining a pool of skilled professionals and your skill is a given, so have it ready. The question, then, is what *else* do you bring? What's unique about you?

That essence, that *you*, is what you must bring to every audition.

Charlie's got his face. You might have a mean sense of humor, a high-pitched voice or a hideous nose. Do you think your uniqueness is weird? Well, maybe it is. It's also the thing that will define your career. You might call it talent, you might call it dumb luck. All I know is it's yours and nobody else's, so you might as well take advantage of it.

I told Roxy her story reminded me of a voice-over coach

I once had. When I read audition copy, the coach said she heard me ask, "Do you want this?" when she wanted to hear me declare, "Look what I've got!"

Every audition is an opportunity to declare, "Look what I've got!" What you've got is what folks are there to see. When I can show the thing I've got that no one else has, I've succeeded. Even if I don't book the job, the casting director will call me in again when there's something right for me.

"I love it!" said Roxy. "'Look what I've got!' I'm going to use it next time I pitch the network."

The potted plant tipped over, revealing Adorable Waiter. "Sorry," he said. "I wanted to hear the end of the story." He limped away to take an order.

Roxy leaned across the table. "You know what he's got besides being adorable? He's a good listener. Handy in this town."

"Look what I've got," I said, grabbing the check. It was worth it.

◆

CHAPTER 7

THE GREEN-EYED MONSTER

I'm rarely jealous of other performers. Yes, it would be nice to have Scarlett Johansson's looks or Kerry Washington's looks or Jennifer Aniston's looks or Lady Gaga's wardrobe budget. But I don't feel jealous of them because I don't know them well enough. I can't feel jealousy from a distance. It's too much work.

Then there's Charlotte. She's one of those people who can do everything. She's a working actor, mother, wife, musician, producer, director, writer and, by god, a shrink. I kid you not. On top of everything else, she's a bona fide, certified therapist.

I don't mean she has at one time in her life been all these things. I mean that she *is* all these things, all at once, right now.

She's also attractive, slim, smart, funny and talented. Most important, she's my friend. She's seen me through some struggles and I've supplied extra backbone when she's needed it. Yet sometimes when she tells me of her latest accomplishment I feel like someone reached into my stomach and squished it with both hands.

I know that doesn't do either of us any good. I also know that when Charlotte tells me of an achievement, she's not doing so to hurt my feelings. She's telling me because she loves me, and we share our joys with the people we love.

Like yesterday on the phone. Charlotte had been out of town and, immediately upon her return, she plunged into a new project which involved networking with famous theater directors from all over the country. It sounded exciting and she was inspired by the work. At the same time, she's got a show opening in a couple of weeks for which she's the musical director. She also produces a night club act where she showcases all kinds of artists, and performs music she's written. She's collaborating on a new musical.

Oh—and I should mention that she has two national commercials running.

And she does yoga and meditates every day. And she's a good cook.

She had to get off the phone to go pick up her (charming, intelligent, well-adjusted) son from a play-date, so I quickly asked the question I'd called about in the first place: I liked her headshot, so I wanted to know who took it.

"I did. I thought it would be fun to try."

She took her own fabulous headshot. A color, digital headshot with perfect lighting. *She took it of herself.* On a *whim*.

Okay, missy, hold it right there. That's enough.

My stomach shouted a big "Wuh-oh!" Competition rose in my belly like bile. It's not just that Charlotte does a million things. It's that she's *good* at all of them.

My jealousy is illogical: most of the things Charlotte does are things I'm not interested in doing. I don't want to write music or direct theater or sit across the desk from fellow neurotics and listen to their tales of woe. So why does this feeling rise up in me?

Maybe it's sheer volume. She does so much.

I can do some things. I can act and write, and I'm a decent photographer. My house is relatively clean. I haven't practiced yoga in a while, but I have a mat. I don't meditate, but I could. I might be able to do other things, you know, if I wanted to try.

And there you have it.

Charlotte has so much energy! Where does she find it? Caffeine can only take you so far. She must be getting up at 4 a.m.!

I am not willing to do that. If I got up at 4 a.m. I'd be down for a nap by noon, and there goes my multi-tasking time. Just today I need to buy gas, replace the filter in the water pitcher and run the dishwasher. Hell, I should congratulate myself. I can do all that and more in a single afternoon and still have time to check my email every twenty minutes.

Jealous? Don't be. We all have our talents. Some people just have more talents than others.

CHAPTER 8
TEST

If art reflects life, then there are lessons to be learned for our daily use. Herein, a few things I'm learning from television (you won't be tested on these):
1. There is no pink, yellow or lime green in a crisis. Likewise, there's no navy blue or slate gray when you're having fun.
2. FBI agents are unable to communicate while standing still. They can speak only while striding, briskly and with determination, along recently-waxed hallways.
3. If you are ever arrested for a crime, you will need a lawyer of either gender who has toned thighs, well-defined biceps and flat abs.
4. Assistant district attorneys and medical interns earn exorbitant salaries, drive late model cars, and have exquisite taste in furniture.
5. Cleavage commands reverence in municipal offices

and courtrooms. (Boobs never go out of style. If you have them, use them.)

6. Women climb the corporate ladder in mini-skirts. Slacks are acceptable upon occasion, but don't forget item 5.
7. Human memory is unclear because filters, soft lights and odd camera angles make it fuzzy.
8. Coroners are sexy. If you want to get laid, head out to the clubs this weekend with a dab of formaldehyde behind your earlobes.
9. Sex is graceful, never messy. Here's why:
   a. all women wear sexy underwear every day (because it's comfortable);
   b. all men have great chests;
   c. no one needs birth control and STDs are imaginary.
10. You do not need to know what to feel. The music will tell you.
11. Script trumps everything, even acting. Except on reality TV, but the rest of the rules apply.

Actually, on that one, you'll be tested.

CHAPTER 9

DESPERATION STINKS

In the great book of demographics I'm listed as a married person, but I was single long enough to have attained an advanced level of expertise on the subject. Among other things, I learned that if you want a deep and loving relationship, you can't allow yourself to want it too much. If you do you might begin to feel desperate, and desperation is the worst way to start a relationship because the potential partner can smell it on you. It's stinky.

The opposite is true, too. As soon as your loneliness ends and you're in a positive, happy relationship, others are drawn to you like flies (talk about stinky!). At last they want you, maybe even desperately, because you're not available.

It's rare for an acting career to resemble actual life, but nevertheless I recommend applying this to your auditions. If you walk into the casting office wanting that job so badly you're salivating, there's no way it's going to be a good audition for you. I don't care if you're the best actor this side of Morgan Freeman. I don't care if your acting can cure the common cold. If you want that job desperately you will *not* get it.

Which suggests that, basically, we have to lie.

Did you move to the big city and take night jobs in data entry and table wiping because you *don't* want to act? Sure, I groveled at the feet of beefy, overpaid men in drab suits because it was fun. I complimented their taste in ties, quietly corrected their spelling and covered for them when their wives called, all while answering to the name "Her," because I enjoyed the humiliation.

It seems impossible to solve the problem of wanting-to-act vs. not-wanting-to-appear-to-want-too-much-to-act. But it can be done. "Not wanting" is a two-step process.

First, you must not need the money.

Second, you must not need the artistic fulfillment.

Not needing an acting job for the money is easy if you have a day job that pays enough to get you through. I recommend you find one that doesn't make you hate yourself every time you punch in, because that only increases your desperation.

Artistic fulfillment is easy, too. In fact, you can get artistic fulfillment by doing a non-paying play in a 99-seat (or, realistically, a 29-seat) theater. You can get artistic fulfillment in a touchy-feely acting class or by performing heart-rending monologues in the shower.

But we're talking about an acting *job* here. One that pays, uh, whaddayacallit?—money. Unless you're on a short list for an Oscar you're probably auditioning either for a commercial or one of those TV roles that provides exposition so the star can react emotionally. Artistic fulfillment is likely not a factor.

So now that you've gotten financial need and artistic fulfillment out of the way, you can achieve comfort and confidence in the audition room. All your suffering and hard work can pay off in an unfulfilling acting job that you don't want or need!

Hurrah…!?

Well, it's going to look great on your résumé. With enough of those babies under your belt, you'll never encounter the desperation question again. And you are going to smell *sooooo* good.

CHAPTER 10

READY

My agent Blanche told me a story over coffee last week. (All of Blanche's stories are told over coffee.) It's about one of her clients who is not, unfortunately, me.

Alicia's been recurring in a small role on a sitcom for a couple of seasons, with a few lines in a few episodes. One recent Monday morning, Blanche got a call from the show's casting director. The star was sick. Would Alicia be willing to stand in for the star at the network read-through? That very day? With only a few hours' notice?

Why, yes. Alicia would.

The network executives wouldn't expect a full performance. They'd be more than grateful if Alicia would just hit the marks and read the lines so they could get an idea of how well the script was working.

"How'd she do?" I asked, while Blanche stirred whipped cream into her café mocha.

"She was brilliant of course," said Blanche. "My phone

started ringing the minute it was over."

The first one to call was the casting director, who said, "Alicia saved my gosh darn butt!" or words to that effect. Then Blanche heard from the head of network casting. Who knew he was in the audience that day? He loved Alicia's work. Blanche told him, "Get her a gosh darn series!" because Blanche is a good agent.

"Is he getting her a series?" I asked.

"I don't know, but she's a 'name' at that network now. And I hear the producer told the writers to write more gosh darn material for her."

I was happy for Alicia. Happy for Blanche, too, because she represents only actors she believes in and it's great when your belief is validated. Apparently we don't always make it easy for her.

"You know, some actors I represent would have turned down that job," she said.

"Seriously?" I spilled a little when my cup landed too hard on the table. "Why?"

"They think it's beneath them to 'understudy.' They wouldn't have taken such a small role to begin with, even though it's recurring. Alicia took it and ran with it. Not bad for an understudy, huh?"

Not bad at all.

I called Alicia the next day. Still high from the experience, she was glad to tell me about it.

When she'd gotten the call that Monday, instinct told her the read-through was an opportunity and she had to be prepared. To her that meant several things. Of course it meant the script, and she only had two hours to study it. The regulars had had it all weekend. Alicia worked hard to be off book, especially for the emotional scenes, even though no one expected that of her.

Although the regulars often show up casually dressed, Alicia decided to carry herself as if she were shooting the episode. Keeping it subtle, she wore her good jeans and a cute top, did her hair and wore make-up, even though no one expected that, either.

Knowing there was no pressure on her to excel, she made a decision: to do just that. That meant full-on acting, even in the kissing scenes.

"You had to kiss?" I asked. Acting-kissing can be so awkward. "Did you know the guy?"

"I had met one of them."

"You kissed more than one guy? In a read-through?"

"They wanted to see how the script was working. It was my job to show them. Plus, I wanted them to see I could be comfortable with the material."

"Were you nervous?"

"Not really. I knew the expectations were low. I wanted to exceed expectations and leave the impression that I was one of them. I belonged there."

I was one of them. I belonged there.

Her words jolted me. Sometimes I've felt out of place on a set. I've thought it was because I was unsure of the routine or I didn't know people. Sometimes I blamed it on them, thinking they were unwelcoming or cliquish. What if it was my own mind-set?

A casting director doesn't hand such an opportunity to just anyone. Alicia was a known quantity. But there were other recurring female actors on the show who might have been chosen, and you can bet they're all good. That's how they got there. So why Alicia?

"Do you know why they picked you to do the read-through?" I asked.

Alicia was too polite to say, so I asked in a different way. "Are you always on time? Do you always go to the set looking good? Do you always know your lines and hit your marks? Are you always easy to work with?"

"Well, it's kind of a no-brainer," Alicia said without pausing. "I mean, why would you do it any other way?"

It could be she's just the right type. Or maybe, out of all the actors to choose from, the casting director was confident that Alicia would make him look the best because she's been laying that track all along. Her preparation the day of the read-through was icing on the cake. She'd already done the most important work. She'd made herself ready by being more than a good actor; she's a professional with a positive attitude. Maybe she hadn't known people were watching, but they were.

"There's something else," said Alicia. "My morning meditation for weeks had been about being on that set in a larger capacity, and having people appreciate what I have to offer. I didn't know what that would be, but I wanted to prep myself for how it would feel. That 'I belong there' feeling."

"It worked," I said, thinking I really ought to start meditating. "How many guys did you have to kiss?"

"Only two," she said. "Too bad, huh?"

So Alicia played the lead before an audience of network executives. She spoke the lines, hit her marks and kept her cool as expected. She also kissed her men, hit the emotional highs, even cried real tears in the moment. In short, she acted. No one expected that.

When it was over there was applause for the cast and hugs for Alicia. Most importantly, Alicia gave herself an inward hug because she had accomplished what she had set out to do.

One could argue that the circumstances were right, which is true. I wonder, though, if Alicia got the call because she was lucky. Maybe. But it didn't hurt that she was also ready. She doesn't have a series yet but it's only a matter of time, because she's right, gosh darn it. She belongs there.

CHAPTER 11
MY INSTRUMENT

We've been hearing it since college acting classes: an actor must take care of his or her "instrument." Our instrument is our self—body, mind, spirit. As artists we must feed it, nurture it, treat it right, keep the instrument in tune. Unlike a rock star, we can't go smashing our instrument in the finale and replacing it with a new one the next night, unless we want lots of plastic surgery in our future.

But oh, the instrument goes through some changes! When you're young it's naturally in tune and doesn't require a lot of attention. You feed it instant ramen and beer for weeks and it continues to play beautiful music. You go through all sorts of trauma just trying to grow up, and still the thing works like the first violin in the L.A. Philharmonic.

But as you get older you have to work harder to keep your instrument well-tuned. Whether you lift weights, do aerobics, run or practice yoga, you have to do lots more of it every year to keep the old trumpet from sounding like a kazoo.

After a certain age, my instrument started needing all kinds of special stuff, like a lumbar support pillow and a middle-of-the-night pee break. I finally cut out dairy because the alternative was incessant hot flashes. I also require an array of vitamins and supplements; they help me stay in tune, but don't ask me how because I can't remember.

I take my instrument hiking, which keeps my heart beating like a drum and keeps my body from looking like one, but my instrument's feet hurt unless I wear orthopedic insoles, so it's a trade-off. High heels are sheer torture, but even when I was twenty, wearing heels was like walking on hot coals.

I see a lot of actors tuning their instruments at coffee shops and I want to shout, "Too much caffeine is bad for you!" except I love caffeine, and now that I'm not getting eight hours of sleep every night, a gulp of caffeine comes in handy to grease the old strings.

The worst thing is that it's becoming more difficult to keep my instrument petite. The violin wants to become a stand-up bass. Sometimes it doesn't know what's good for it, insisting on cookies when what it really needs is a carrot. But even as a young instrument it didn't much care for carrots.

Maybe aging is just part of moving forward in our careers. You start out as the ingénue/love interest, then you're the young mommy/love interest, then suddenly you're the love interest's mother. Pretty soon you're playing lawyers, doctors and neighbors. That's me right now. It won't be long before I'm the ingénue/love interest's grandmother, if I'm lucky. Those parts are few and far between.

Growing older forces us to evolve, to learn to play a new set of roles. It's like teaching a stringed instrument to blow like a horn. That's true in any profession.

Good things come to the aging actor: confidence, experience, acceptance. Perhaps I'm not a brand new violin, but as long as I stay in tune I'm a classic Stradivarius, which is a lot more valuable.

◉

CHAPTER 12
EXCUSES

My dog ate my sides.
I ran out of gas and had to hitchhike to the audition.
My return flight from the moon was delayed and they were out of dehydrated peanuts.

Your audition is less than brilliant and you have a great excuse. Does it matter? Is there such a thing as a good excuse for giving less than your best?

Friday audition time: 3 p.m.: I've worked the sides to death, made my choices, researched the show and planned my outfit.

Friday, 1 p.m.: I slip my sides into clear plastic sleeves so they'll stay dry. I hang them in the shower for a final, un-dress rehearsal.

Yes, I do that. Would I kid you? I *must* do it. *It's my routine.*

Friday, 1:02 p.m.: No hot water.

My heroic husband Socrates ventures to the basement underworld and returns with a report: the water heater has burst and we have a two-inch flood. Socrates is a genius but his knowledge base does not include household repairs.

I'm about to meet a new casting director who wants to see me act like the distraught mother of a murder victim. I must audition in a heightened emotional state with real tears and perfect hair. I cannot achieve either of these with a cold shower.

Socrates calls a plumber. I call the neighbors. They're accommodating, but I can hardly hang up my sides and rehearse at the top of my lungs in *their* shower. My routine is ruined. I barely make it to the audition and my work is only passable. If it doesn't stick in the casting director's mind as the worst she's ever seen that's because it won't stick in her mind at all.

I could've nailed that scene if our water heater hadn't blown up. Plus people were chatting outside the audition room and they distracted me! Not to mention there's gum on the bottom of my shoe, the neighbor's cat is in heat and the Cubs are having a pretty good season. How am I supposed to concentrate?

Well, that's *my* problem, isn't it?

The casting director doesn't care. She needs the best person for the job, and if I'm not it it doesn't matter why, at least not to her. If there's an earthquake and the office falls down around us, the job's going to go to the actor who doesn't notice, or who finds a way to use the crumbling building as their character's motivation.

Making excuses to the casting director is like making excuses to myself. If I get off track it's up to me to find a way to get back on. Maintaining concentration isn't easy but no one's going to do it for me, and if I sit in the waiting room thinking of reasons I can't succeed, I'll find them. So I might as well sit there thinking of reasons to shine.

A broken water heater is not an excuse. Getting the sides at the last minute is not an excuse. Traffic is not an excuse. I'm rackin' my brains here, and I can't come up with a good excuse to do a bad audition.

Are you sick? Did a loved one die? Did you get rear-ended? These aren't excuses so much as reasons not to show up in the first place. Some people can do it under those circumstances. Hey, if you can beat that stress, hell yes! Go and book that job as soon as the paramedics finish tying off your splint. But if you can't, give yourself a break. Call your agent and cancel. He'll understand. Because even if you have an excuse for auditioning below top form, it doesn't matter. You still don't get the part.

As for the water heater—did you know plumbers are booked farther into the future than a Montessori school? To avoid overburdening our goodwill with the neighbors, we bought a camp shower and hung it from a tree in the back yard. We allow the sun to heat the water during the day, and shower at night for the privacy of darkness. I can't see my sides in the dark. My routine is ruined and my audition prep is a total shambles. I've had to adapt.

A few days ago I auditioned for the role of a rich socialite. My emotional prep was especially tough; how many wealthy sophisticates do you know who wash their armpits in the sink?

I booked it. A good casting director can smell the right actor the minute she walks in the door.

◆

CHAPTER 13

PRIMAL SCENE

The church my family attended in our medium-sized, Midwestern town held an annual mother/daughter banquet. Every woman was expected to volunteer. My mother was a teacher and breadwinner before the feminist movement gave her permission; it wasn't like her to make a casserole or decorate the church basement. She was a writer and had studied acting in college, so instead of baking a cake or hanging crepe paper she wrote a play for the two of us to perform at the event.

I was five years old, so she wrote a simple piece. A mother and daughter do the dishes. The mother washes, the daughter dries. The daughter asks a lot of questions about God. The mother doesn't have all the answers.

I learned to memorize lines at age five because my mother taught me how. I learned to project my voice because she took me to the church and we practiced in the basement, where the banquet would be held. Mother stood in the back of the room, and we called our lines out to each other across the expanse until I could hear her and she could hear me. She taught me to breathe from my diaphragm, and to enunciate so I could be understood.

Mother taught me simple stage tools like cheating out, how not to upstage her or to be upstaged by her, even how to hold for a laugh without breaking character.

But she didn't teach me to work with props. At one point, the daughter breaks a dish and learns that mistakes are part of life. We had dishtowels, but we didn't have a lot of dishes to waste so we didn't practice breaking one. We figured we'd just do that in the show.

The church basement had a pale green tile floor and green-painted cinder block walls, with windows high at the top that let in the outdoor light. In the early evening of banquet night after the sun went down, fluorescent lights gave the cavernous room a sepia glow.

In the stainless steel kitchen, some of the mothers had prepared a meal of macaroni and cheese casserole, green beans and a salad of iceberg lettuce with Italian dressing. We served ourselves, ate our macaroni from paper plates and drank lemonade out of paper cups. Women and girls sat on metal folding chairs at portable tables.

After dinner, Mother and I climbed the three steps to the small stage. I was nervous but not terribly so, because I didn't know what it would be like to perform for an audience. I wore a tan and black striped shift Mother had made for me. Mother wore Capri pants and a white blouse. Her dark brown hair was in the swept-up do she wore when she was young.

Mothers shushed their daughters until there was silence.

Soon, the scraping of metal chairs on tile ceased. Our audience waited. I looked out over pointed eyeglasses, puffy hairdos and red fingernails. I remember Mary Janes, white anklets and dirty knees. The moms and daughters gazed up at us, their fluorescent-lit faces attentive. They knew that even if it was boring, at least it wouldn't last forever.

Mother said her first line. I answered with mine, too quietly. She spoke again, louder, her voice guiding me to focus. I remembered to enunciate and speak up.

Then something happened that none of us had expected. Mother and I got involved in our conversation. Even though we were speaking memorized lines, projecting and cheating out, we talked to each other. I heard her words as though for the first time, and my responses were new to us both. But the play was only a few minutes long; we didn't realize what was happening until the dish slipped out of my hands and shattered on the cement floor of the stage.

It shocked Mother. It even shocked me. The audience gasped.

We had believed.

In the moment, my five-year-old self felt the power of holding an audience. Yes, I believed, but it was *their* belief that hooked me.

Maybe I made it up. Could I have been that young? There are later events in my life that I don't remember as clearly. Could I have told the story to myself so many times that I've created details?

The moment of the broken plate is primal for me. I try to find it again and again. On stage, on sound stages, even in casting offices, I try to break that plate and hold others in my moment.

There's something more, something my mother knew then that I didn't know: it's through our brokenness that we find our art. In glib terms we call it "getting in touch with our emotions." It means experiencing the love and pain of our lives and allowing ourselves to bring that to our work. Did my mother expect my five-year-old self to grasp that? I doubt it, but she's no longer here to ask. Her dark, swept-up hair grew silver, and when she died we boxed up her writings along with her dishes and mementoes. Somewhere in my garage is a copy of the little play she wrote for us to share.

CHAPTER 14

AN ENSEMBLE CREW

A good production crew has been called a well-oiled machine. It's true, though I have yet to see a machine with such a variety of facial hair, such a wry sense of humor, or such a vast collection of T-shirts.

When I began working in Hollywood, crews were made up of grizzled guys of all ages with ponytails, muscles, tool belts and cutoffs. Even the women suffered from testosterone overload. Now pretty women can crew (they're the ones with the ponytails now), and everyone wears baggy cargo shorts with infinite pockets. As for T-shirts, if the idea of jail were not so distasteful I'd spend my entire lunch break reading chests.

Time and experience together make a crew efficient. But their tasks are defined by union rules and job descriptions, so even without time together, if everyone does what's required the crew works like that well-oiled machine.

Actors have job descriptions, too, though sometimes

ours are not as specific as those of the crew. Our union contracts, professional experience and director define what we're expected to do: know our lines, hit our marks, pay attention, etc. That can mean three things or three hundred. Each job is different and we don't know until we get there exactly what it's going to be. So besides our job skills we need energy, patience and something extra: etiquette. Like, you know, being polite.

I had the good fortune to work on a commercial last week. The job was huge; the director had 18 spots to shoot in 5 days, with 45 principals, countless extras and a massive crew. My spot was third to shoot on the second day, and we started ahead of schedule.

Ahead of schedule.

My theory is that this bizarre turn of events occurred because the director was respectful, crew members were courteous and actors were alert and responsive. Folks said things like "please" and "thank you" and "excuse me." They did that etiquette thing.

For my spot, seven of us stuffed ourselves into a tiny office cubicle. The director moved us around until he was happy with the arrangement. Those of us in the rear stood on apple boxes and those in front crouched down so the camera could see everyone. It was far less than comfortable, but we engaged our senses of humor, tried not to poke each other in the wrong places and got the shot done quickly.

Off the set during a break, we stayed out of the crew's way while they set up the next shot. Background actors and principals mixed, swapping stories and advice. Everyone was amazed and not a little surprised at how well it was going. Conversation turned to situations where things hadn't worked so well.

"I've been on jobs where people shoved each other to be in front of the camera," one actor said.

"That's happened to me at auditions."

"Me too. I know this guy who…"

Everyone has a story about bad behavior on the set. It's not the norm. In fact it's so rare it's a shock when it happens, which is why you remember. Apparently casting directors remember, too; we noticed the pushers and shovers were not on the job with us.

While I watched the crew move lights and wrangle cords with practiced efficiency, I wondered: what if they decided to shove each other out of the way to do whatever they pleased? Suppose the production assistant decided she wanted to be key grip? Explosions guaranteed! If the set designer preferred to fix lunch, the food would probably look fabulous but taste of paint and plaster. And wardrobe chosen by the gaffer might be interesting, but I don't want him touching my hair.

As one of the make-up staff powdered my nose for the next shot, she said, "We've had mostly good actors. In two days, only two jerks."

Casting directors do their best to weed out the—well, the weeds, but some slip by. It's no matter. The second A.D. keeps a list for future reference, assuming she isn't busy operating the boom.

The actors in my group were finished long before rush hour began. We said "good-bye, enjoyed working with you," etc., and we meant it. Actors tend to bond on jobs. Whether we're working together for weeks in a play or a film, or just a day on a commercial, it's natural (for those of us who don't shove) to become an ensemble.

Bonding must surely be as natural for crew members as it is for actors, but there's no time for the crew to chat on a fast job like that. They have time only for the please-and-thank-you stuff. So as we left we thanked the crew members who were still around. Most were already off to the next location with another spot to shoot before they headed home.

Compared to what that crew was up against, it was an easy job for us actors. The crew faced three more days of multiple spots and not all were set in air-conditioned offices. I hope they had polite actors to work with. They deserved no less. They were nice to us but of course it was only day two.

Good set etiquette is oil to the machine. In fact, "Play Nice" would make a perfect T-shirt logo for my lunch break reading.

"Excuse me, I think you're the very best boy! Mind if I read your chest?"

CHAPTER 15

MY FEEL-GOOD AUDITION SONG

Horror of horrors! There are days when I don't want to act!

Oh, admit it. You have them, too.

It's not because I'm jaded. Some days I just wake up that way. I'm not in the mood. I could be auditioning to sell adult diapers or in the middle of a run of *Antony and Cleopatra,* it doesn't matter. At times I simply don't feel like putting myself out there.

It's no big deal when items such as "do laundry," "walk Phiz" and "clean the refrigerator" fill my calendar. I can delight in those activities whether I feel like acting or not. But acting isn't some drudge paycheck where you can hide behind a computer screen and snore through the day on automatic pilot. When you audition you've got to bring energy and enthusiasm even if you have to manufacture them.

That's where my secret weapon comes in. It's a song.

I don't waste the song on times when listening to the radio or psyching myself up with a pep talk will do. I play my song only when all other methods have been exhausted—when, after I've tried everything, I'd still prefer farm labor, scrubbing floors or even phone sales to getting my hopes up one more time and acting my heart out for 90 seconds in a casting office.

If I'm already heading to the audition I pull over (because it's an emergency), plug in my phone and select the song. The piano notes tinkle. I smile. Then the bass joins in and my body recognizes the tune. My tension lets out in a sigh. The guitar starts strumming and my smile opens up. My neck and shoulders relax and I laugh out loud. I'm ready to get back on the road.

My audition song never fails. If anyone saw me driving along they'd change lanes and call the cops, because by the time the lyrics kick in I've turned the volume to full blast, my free arm is waving, I've loosened up into total boogie and I can barely keep my foot on the pedal.

Sing it with me!

"There's a road I'd like to tell you 'bout, lives in my home town..."

Yep. It's the sweet, hippie harmonies of—you guessed it—Aliotta, Haynes and Jeremiah, singing "Lake Shore Drive."

You didn't guess it?

That's because it's my song. It works for me. You're going to have to find your own.

"Lake Shore Drive" is perhaps obscure if you're not from the Midwest. It isn't a song about acting. Frankly, the lyrics make a subtle reference to using LSD, a "feel-good" state for which I'm not particularly nostalgic. The cover of the 25th anniversary CD sports a black and white photograph of three shirtless guys with bushy mustaches and 1970s hair, showing off matching tattoos and bedroom eyes. Man, they were cool back in the day. And I've changed so much since then.

But the song transports me to my youthful Chicago days when everything was before me and my dreams were big. My career and most of my life lay ahead. When I hear the song now I'm reminded that I'm still filled with hope, not just for my career but for everything. There's so much to come.

If you don't have your own audition song already you'll find one eventually, or one will find you. I never expected "Lake Shore Drive" to be mine. Anyone who knows me would have thought it was more likely to be "Stairway to Heaven" or "King of Pain," or even "What Kind of Fool Am I?"

But "Lake Shore Drive" it is, and it's a sweet tune. Next time you hear it, if it's not coming from your own stereo and you see some wacko driving by, don't worry about changing lanes. It may not look like it, but I've got it under control. I've got an audition and I'm in the mood to act.

"Just you and your mind and Lake Shore Drive, tomorrow is another day,

And the sunshine's fine in the morning time, tomorrow is another day..."

Piano, fiddle, (woo!), fade...

◆

CHAPTER 16
INNER BOHEMIAN

The other day I had a voice-over, two auditions and tickets to a friend's play, all scattered across the Southland in a schedule that defied space and time as we know it. In a downpour of morning rain I loaded three different outfits into the car, because each audition required a different wardrobe and neither of my audition outfits was appropriate for an evening at the theater. I packed my briefcase with make-up, jewelry, snacks and reading material. The floor of the car looked like a shoe store.

If you've never driven in L.A., here's a tip for future reference: when it rains here people drive as though a) it's not rain but sleet, b) sleet is a new experience, and c) they're either 17 and drunk or 96 and blind.

I was late to my voice-over, which made the session run overtime. When I finished, I changed in the bathroom at the studio. Then I dashed off to my first audition, where there was a technical glitch and the best take didn't get recorded.

We had to do it again, which was only one of the things that pushed my schedule to the limit. I ran to the car in the rain, wasted time deciding where to get lunch, made the wrong decision, and waited in line at a busy restaurant to get my food to go.

The sleet—um—rain made it especially necessary to concentrate, and I didn't dare eat while driving. (I'm the 96-and-blind type, it's like I've forgotten everything I learned in Chicago.) I was almost late to my second audition and I had to leave my lunch in the car.

At the second casting office I hurried to change in the bathroom. Lucky me, they were running behind, so after all the rushing I had time to cool my overheated heels. The place was packed: a humid corral filled with sheep waiting for the slaughter, while casting assistants called out names. I finally got to audition, and when I finished I hauled my butt to the Valley to see my friend's show.

By that time the freeways were a complete loss so I made a heroic yet foolish attempt to be on time by taking surface streets. In addition to the rain, long stretches of several Hollywood streets were blocked in advance of the Academy Awards. I'd forgotten; half of Hollywood had been closed for weeks to set up security, bleachers, and those big, gold statues. Traffic slithered like a reptile in the swamp. The defroster wasn't much help so I cracked open the back windows, taking care not to allow rain on my clothing rack or my mobile shoe store. I finally got to the Valley at about 7:30, found a parking spot, ate my cold lunch and changed clothes in the car.

It was a great day. An absolute blast.

For one thing I had a job, which by itself made it worth risking the freeway in the rain. And the recording studio people forgave my lateness. I wasn't the only one who had to find a way around the Awards and the rain to get there.

And my first audition, yeah, the take I liked was lost. But the assistant caught the glitch, the other actors generously stepped aside so my partner and I could try again, and what do I know? Maybe the second take was the best one after all. My audition partner was terrific and it turns out we have mutual friends. And get this: the script wasn't the usual crap.

The casting director at the second audition had her dog with her. If you ask me, dogs make every situation better. The place was full of interesting people and, since the session was running behind, I had time not only to chat but to study the copy. Which, believe it or not, was also not crap.

(You think I'm lying. Two commercial auditions in one day, and decent copy at both of them. I'd think it was a lie, too, if I hadn't seen it. Stranger than fiction.)

When my commercial agent apologized for loading me with two auditions 15 miles and ten minutes apart on the one day I had a job, I thanked her. Apologize for two auditions? I love days when my car is my dressing room/office/lounge. I suppose I'm still an actor when I'm home twiddling my thumbs, but I feel more like the real thing when I'm out pounding the pavement. The more literally, the better.

I managed to knock back an espresso before my friend's show, though I didn't need it because the show was good enough to keep me awake. The day's only bad moment: there is no way to redeem cold French fries.

My favorite part of the day, the thing that topped two auditions and even a job, was changing clothes in my parked car. It's a tight space—the car as well as the pants—but I managed with wriggling and grunting. I allowed the windows to steam up and the passersby to use their imaginations, creating my own evening of performance art.

My inner bohemian lives on.

CHAPTER 17
GLAD TO BE HERE

Everywhere I looked was a female face topped with short, salt-and-pepper hair. We each wore a tasteful, light blue blouse and khakis. Not too much makeup. Midwestern types that people could relate to. Everywhere was another me. It was a hall of mirrors.

Or maybe it was a commercial audition.

But throw a bunch of women into a tight space and let 'em simmer a while. If you can't see their differences, you'll hear them.

I avoid the complainers. They're the ones who swear under their breath: "It's #^@&ing rude to make us wait like this," and "These a**holes don't know what they're doing" and "God, I hate auditions." That negative stuff rubs off, and I don't want it all over me when I get in front of the camera.

I avoid the chatters, too, which isn't easy because I often run into friends at auditions. Today I saw someone I'd been in a play with a couple of years ago. We caught up, then we both said, "Nice seeing you, let's split up so we can work on our copy." She's a pro. Most people are.

I found a corner to hide in. I had so much time to work on that copy I memorized it with about thirty variations.

When I finally got into the audition room I discovered the holdup: one assistant, new on the job, was running the session by himself. He was sweating, harried and trying so hard to do everything right that he was shaking. There were enough empty coffee cups littering the room to serve the entire staff of Disney Studios, and it was only 11:30.

"Sorry about the wait," he said, twitching as he took my headshot. His cheeks were as red as his hair.

"It's okay, it's part of the job."

He laughed really loud, which was weird because what I said wasn't funny. But I think he needed the relief. "That's cool," he said. "A lot of these women have somewhere else they want to be."

Well, sure. Me too. There are plenty of places I'd rather be than in a hot audition room, reading copy from cue cards some terrified kid has so painstakingly drawn up for me. I'd rather be on the actual job, for example, saying the lines for real. Or on a massage table, spending part of my paycheck. Or maybe Paris, spending the whole damn thing plus a few years' worth of residuals from the huge, national ad campaign, of which I am the star.

But it's 11:30 on a weekday. Other people are loading trucks, selling cars, serving coffee, performing surgery, typing memos, picking strawberries, teaching classes, cleaning bedpans, painting houses, giving manicures, dusting crops, driving locomotives or setting up circus tents. *This* is what I do for a living, and out of the thousands of actors in Los Angeles who would love to be auditioning, I'm actually doing it. I'm glad to be here.

I don't know if my "glad to be there" attitude showed on camera. I think it did, but I don't care. I don't care if the job went to the bitchiest woman at the audition. I'm just glad I don't have to go through life hating my work as much as some of those women did.

Sometimes casting runs behind. The office is understaffed. Traffic is bad. Somebody's sick. The client took a long lunch and set the schedule back. Or maybe the casting director really is a jerk. Who knows? It happens. I can't change it by complaining. The best I can do is leave time for screw-ups and go with the flow. Auditioning is a huge percentage of what I do. I spend too much time at it to allow it to be something I hate.

The business is tough enough. If you don't love it—if you don't even like it—why put yourself through it?

CHAPTER 18
DROP EVERYTHING

An email arrived today from my theatrical agent, Blanche:

guys: please bring pictures w/resumes ASAP

ATTACH the resumes please I shouldn't have to tell you

ellen—you have only one pic left and I've called you twice

mike—where are short hair shots love the haircut but we have only long hair shots you said they'd be here last week

petrea—business suit shot is out also low on other shots

dave—we've been out of shots for a long time hon

AGGHHH! DROP EVERYTHING! CALL THE PRINTER! CANCEL THE DENTIST! NO DOG WALK! WE'RE HAVING LEFTOVERS! BLANCHE NEEDS HEADSHOTS!

I took a deep breath, then exhaled and emailed Blanche.

Thanks for letting me know. I'll drop off headshots tomorrow, résumés attached.

Next came a frenzy of searching for my headshots in my photo program, clicking around my computer files trying to find and update my résumé, and printing, printing, printing. Then I heard a tiny "ding." I had a new email from Blanche.

if only everyone was as conscientious as you

Blanche has no room in her schedule for capital letters or punctuation. Thank goodness she can spell.

I wondered, though, about Dave, another person on her list. Blanche and I go back to our Chicago days. I know a lot of her clients. Dave's a friend, and he's even more conscientious than I am, if you can believe that. (Okay, you can.) Dave's organized, punctual, dutiful—the steadfast, sensible type. He wouldn't have to search his files or update his résumé because he'd have everything ready to go. I was intrigued. I clicked "reply."

What's up with Dave?

Blanche's response:

omg poor dave has had a time of it at his uncle's funeral he accidentally got his finger closed in the door of the hearse and it drove off he is now without the tip of his pinkie more a problem commercially than theatrically and when he got home his girlfriend had moved out just doesn't live in the apt anymore no explanation very weird also his car is gone he lost it simply lost it thinks it was stolen but it was a piece of crap so that's impossible all of this in a single week so money is a big problem right now among other things poor guy

when you bring your pics tomorrow bring me a double shot mocha will you

oh and he got fired

Wow. I hadn't known any of this. Dave probably hasn't had time to call. Been out looking for his car.

I've often said if you don't have headshots in L.A. you're not an actor. No excuses. But Dave might have proven me wrong.

We've all been told over and over again that acting must come first. I used to believe it. I still drop everything for an audition. That's the nature of the work. As is true of any business, we have to jump when opportunities arise.

But actors carry additional pressures. In other businesses, you're not applying for a new job every day. We must always be in acting class, always be ready with headshots, always keep our wardrobe up-to-the-minute, keep our hair perfect and never step out in public looking less than fabulous.

I follow these rules to the letter. Say, to about F.

The pressure to be at the top of our game at every moment is enormous. But keeping up with the stars on a waiter's budget is just plain unfeasible. Sometimes you have to direct your energies elsewhere. Sometimes the business is not top priority.

Dave's life needs his attention right now. Under his current circumstances, I think he should give Blanche a call (if his phone service hasn't been cut off) and ask for time and understanding. He needs to take care of his finger, get a new job, clean out his ex-girlfriend's closet and find his car. Blanche will understand. Most agents are human. (That's a guess. I don't know most agents. But they know even dedicated actors need the occasional sanity break.)

Blanche hasn't figured out how to use the blind copy function in her email program. I'm tempted to send notes to Ellen and Mike and ask them why they made a busy agent ask twice for headshots. Of course they have my email address, too, so I won't. But I might call Dave and ask if he has time to let me buy him lunch.

I hit "reply" and sent one more note to Blanche.

How about giving Dave a break until he catches up? He's as conscientious as I am. Maybe more.

Her answer was short and sweet.

you know dave he just called we're cool see you tomorrow with that double shot mocha

AGGHHH! TOMORROW! DROP EVERYTHING!

CHAPTER 19

NOR HAM NOR BACON

There has long been disagreement about the identity of William Shakespeare. "Who really wrote the plays?" people ask. Much controversy exists and the evidence is confusing. Could a small-town boy have been so talented, so brilliant, so educated, so worldly? Why, no! It must have been someone else, someone more wealthy, more privileged. Certainly not an *actor*. An *actor* could never have written with such genius.

It's elitist, if you ask me. I know plenty of well-educated actors from small towns who write great stuff. Think Tina Fey. Think Ben Affleck. Think Zach Braff.

(Okay, Ben's from Boston, which is a big town. Okay, I don't know any of these people. But you get my drift.)

It's plausible enough that the author was good old Will. What I find difficult to believe is that he was an actor. Where's the evidence? Very little survives. You see his name on the occasional cast list but there are no cover letters to casting directors, no business cards or post cards. Since we're talking about Elizabethan times and the smaller world of the London stage as opposed to international cinema, the lack of evidence would not faze me, except for one fact: William Shakespeare didn't have a headshot.

Google "Shakespeare portrait" and you'll get millions of results. There are several portraits in question but only two have been proven to be authentic, and both are posthumous.

If Shakespeare had been an actor, he would have paid good money to have excellent portraits painted on a regular basis. He would have made sure the picture wasn't too glamorous or too young-looking. He would have posed in clothes that were fashionable but not faddish, something that enhanced his appearance but didn't call attention to itself. He would have used a painter who was able to capture his essence, so the powers among London's theatre elite would know exactly what he looked like and what parts he was right for.

And, some 400 years later, we would know which portrait was Shakespeare's because *his name and contact information would be written on it*, right in front.

Yes, he was a company member. If you needed to find him you could contact the production office of The King's Men, the Swan or the Globe. But a busy casting director didn't have time for chasing actors across the maze of Elizabethan London, and Will would have known that. Surely there were other scruffy, medium-sized, slightly balding men around town who would have loved to tread the boards. If Will was an actor, he couldn't afford not to be easily available.

So I think William Shakespeare was exactly who the Stratford-Upon-Avon brochures tell us he was: a great writer who did some acting if and when it was necessary. If he had been as much an actor as he was a writer, he'd have been famous for it. And I guarantee you there would be no doubt about his portrait.

CHAPTER 20
YOU PERSEVERE

I was a golden girl in grade school and junior high, confident of my smarts and acting talent, popular enough to have enemies. When I announced I would become a star, everyone knew I'd make it happen.

But a load of shock and heartbreak packed into a small amount of time can change a person in ways she won't understand for years to come. By college, when I said I was going to be a star, everyone (including me) laughed and said, "Yeah, like *that's* going to happen."

In a brief time, I had experienced a series of traumas including a violent assault, a parent's alcoholism, family drama and a close friend's grisly death. I hadn't understood or even noticed the changes these events created in me, but it was all enough to squish my confidence flat. I no longer believed in my talent. I was afraid to reach too high.

For some reason, though, I persevered.

Certain I couldn't compete, I didn't attempt an acting

major in college. But because I loved the theater and wasn't ready to give up on it, I minored in it. I got a rhetoric degree to fall back on (because there are so many jobs in rhetoric), then moved to Chicago. Chicago was close to home. New York and Los Angeles were too daunting.

I got a job in the office at The Second City Theater in Chicago. I took their improvisation classes. Eventually I found the nerve to audition. The first time around I didn't get the job. But with my second audition, they hired me for the touring company. It was most encouraging.

Soon I auditioned for other theaters. Sometimes I got hired, sometimes not. Despite my lack of confidence I wanted to act and couldn't see myself doing anything else. I didn't know then that confidence was a requirement for the stardom I sought. I thought all I needed was talent, and remembered once having had some.

Brick by brick, I built my career. As I did so I learned to love my art, and the desire to be a good actor began to take precedence over the need for fame. Slowly, deliberately, I found my confidence and put my personality back together, as though I were building a home for myself. It's an apt analogy.

I haven't had what anyone would call a meteoric rise, but here it is more than thirty years later and I've been a working actor a good part of the time.

It isn't all I've wanted. I wanted to be more than a working actor; I wanted to be a great actor. I wanted to be the Maggie Smith of my generation, or the Helen Mirren or the Meryl Streep. But Meryl Streep is the Meryl Streep of my generation. I'm not as successful as she is for one simple reason: I'm not as good an actor as she is.

I wouldn't have admitted that twenty years ago, or I would have made excuses, and I'm a better actor now than I was then. There's a freedom in Streep, to do and to be, a bravery that I continue to seek but haven't achieved.

Yet I've become other things I hadn't known I could be, including self-knowing, happy, fulfilled. These things hold more value for me than stardom. Years ago I didn't know what they were worth because I didn't know how they felt.

I tell you all this because I wonder if any of it sounds familiar to you.

I once thought my past sufferings were unique. But everyone experiences trauma, even Meryl Streep. We get past the pain and let it go. Then we use it. Our misfortunes shape us into the adults we become, the artists we are now. The drama class stars we were as kids were sweet, but a child is unformed. A lack of heartbreak in one's growth makes for a bland adult actor.

Violence and dysfunction in my youth broke my confidence. Maybe your experience marred you physically, or stole your time. What will shape you now is how you use that experience. And you are going to use it, one way or another. An unhappy person uses trauma as something on which to blame her failures. An artist uses it as a source of inspiration. I know this because I started as the one and became the other.

Anyone can be a celebrity; witness reality TV. A need for stardom without art can be neurotic. Stardom used wisely can be a career tool for an artist. And an artist can be fulfilled without stardom.

So. You persevere.

CHAPTER 21
LETHARGY

Sometimes I get sick of being an actor.

Don't get me wrong, acting is what I love. It's not like I'm looking for a new profession (unless it's one that includes an outrageous salary and benefits and requires absolutely nothing of me). But sometimes I don't want to do it. Any of it. Just for today I don't want to pick out headshots or mail post cards to casting directors. I don't want to memorize a monologue or read a script or drive to an audition or even actually act. I want to lie in the sun and drink iced tea and read a book. A book about anything but acting.

I experience this lethargy from time to time. Sometimes the mood lasts a day, sometimes it lasts a week or even a month. It can reach monumental proportions (or perhaps I should say minimal), which would be fine if I didn't need to make a living. But as we all know our careers need constant attention. There's no one out there motivating us but ourselves.

I used to think I was a terrible person for having such feelings. I thought I must not be a real artist if I ever went through a single moment lacking the desire to practice my art, and there may be some truth in that. Surely, to be a star you have to have incredible drive or at least incredible luck. Of course I'm only guessing. If I knew what it took to be a star I'd be a star, if it didn't require too much effort.

But I can still call myself an artist even if I need an occasional break. Art needs renewal. Art needs to do something stupid every once in a while. Art needs to hang out at the beach, drink too many beers and eat a whole bag of potato chips. As a matter of fact, lately Art seems to need to give up on diet and exercise altogether. Art's been sleeping late, surfing the web, avoiding errands and enjoying one bonbon too many. Something's gotta give, and I'd prefer it be something other than the button on Art's jeans.

When there's a paycheck involved it's easy to find motivation. But when that paycheck is a "maybe" far down the road—when there's no immediate, tangible result—it's harder to get motivated. Creativity can be its own reward. I experience that more often than not. But after a while, amusing myself with my talent gets old. I need to amuse someone else, which means I need to find the chutzpah to send out some post cards or take a class or at least dial the phone.

It sounds easy, but sometimes I just can't make myself do it. How do you push yourself when yourself won't budge (especially if yourself has been crammed full of burritos and beer)? How do you manufacture enthusiasm? I've tried everything. I've tried napping, eating snacks, getting a massage—I've even tried reading a cheap novel. Nothing seems to work.

It's been a long week of doing nothing. Well, I did do a few things, the empty refrigerator is evidence of that. Today I'm going to try something new to see if it motivates me. I'm going to attempt to buy a week's worth of groceries with the lack of paycheck that my lack of enthusiasm has earned. Maybe that'll remind me that the one person responsible for my career is me.

CHAPTER 22
RELENTLESSLY LOOPY

WARNING: I have a song in my head and I'm going to tell you what it is. It has been in my head for days. It's not even a whole song. It's part of a song that repeats itself in a relentless loop. I can't get rid of it. Pardon me if it's one of your favorites, but I've come to loathe it so much that I hesitate to admit I know it.

Honey!
(de de de de dink dink)
Aw, Sugar Sugar
(de de de de dink dink)
You are my candy girl, and you've got me wanting you.

Sorry, but I did warn you.

I could play some music and replace it with another song. But soon I would loathe that one, too. I get riffs stuck in my head all the time. Usually it's something that doesn't require attention—like a soundtrack playing under scenes of daily life. The more inane the song the more entrenched it becomes, but even the occasional classical measure gets into my mind and repeats itself until something worse comes along.

I'm not the only one who suffers from this. My husband Socrates used to mention it sometimes until I infected him with a bad case of *Oh, oh oh oh oh, you don't have to go, oh oh oh oh...* We now have a rule in our house that we're not allowed to share on this particular subject.

Does everyone experience this?

Do I have to have a song in my head all the time?

Do other people have songs in their heads all the time?

Does the problem influence our work? Stanley Kubrick had a variety of interesting stuff on his mind when he directed *A Clockwork Orange*. But what the hell was Martin Brest's brain singing during *Gigli*? *Duh doo doo doo, duh da, da, da, that's all I want to say to you...*

It's a good thing we can't hear each others' mental soundtracks or life would be difficult to bear. Imagine an audition where you're trying to inject passion into the copy in spite of *aw, Sugar Sugar,* and all the while the casting director sits behind her desk, tapping her toes to *In-a-gadda-da-vida, baby, don't you know...*

You're right. Casting directors are generally younger than that.

Okay, so she's swaying side to side to the beat of *ring around the rosy, a pocket full of*—just kidding, they're not *that* young—*You know I could take you (I could take you...) I could take you (I could take you...) Shorty I could take you there...*

On the job it would be worse. The grip wrangles the cords

and *it's all right, it's all right, it's all right, she moves in mysterious ways.* The director tears his hair out, not because the scene isn't working, but because he's *being followed by a moonshadow, moonshadow moonshadow.* The boom guy struggles to hear over the recurring strains of *do be do be dooo, do do do dee dah.*

I don't even want to think about the grocery store. People would stroll the aisles, reading labels and choosing items, and all the while there's a cacophony of jingles running through each and every head so loudly that nobody can hear the muzak. That's the only plus I can come up with.

Ding dong, the witch is dead! Which old witch? The wicked witch!

Can you tell me how to get, how to get to Sesame Street?

Five eight eight, two three hundred, EMPIIIIIIIIIIRE!

It's terrifying. You can hear everything from "Nessun Dorma" to "Big Ole Butt"— and that's just *my* head. It's a good thing I'm not a casting director.

I hope Socrates won't be humming when I get home but I know him too well. Whatever it is, I pray it has no lyrics. More likely, though, with my luck it'll be:

Honey!
(de de de de dink dink)
Aw, Sugar Sugar
(de de de de dink dink)
You are my candy girl, and you've got me wanting you.

Let's hope for that. It could be worse.

◉

CHAPTER 23

SAYING IT FORWARD

Tough customer. Vicious villain. Tyrant. I can't wait to play the part.

If it were a theatrical audition we'd be working on our sides. But it's a commercial. Just a look, no lines. Yet in this waiting room, everyone's practicing. Usually when you have a long wait for a commercial audition there's chatter, camaraderie. Women like to talk to each other. But not here. The women are frowning, avoiding eye contact, snubbing each other.

I know we're all preparing, but how hard do you have to practice being a bitch? I can turn it on at a moment's notice.

After half an hour my spirits flag. I'm bored. I should have brought a magazine. I know it's not the responsibility of the other actors in the room to entertain me, but how am I going to play a power-mad villain when I feel like a lukewarm dishrag? I'm just about to march outside to perk up in the hundred-degree heat when a pretty redhead sits across from me and smiles. "I love your suit," she says. "You look great."

Oh! A breath of fresh air! And the chat begins: from "Don't dye your hair, it's great!" to "Have you been auditioning much lately?" to "You're too young to have a son in college. Pics or it didn't happen." Soon we're becoming friends.

I'm showing a photo of my son—er, dog, Phiz, to my red-haired friend when she's called in for her audition.

"You made my day," I say, putting my phone away. "Break a leg!" For a second it crosses my mind that we're supposed to be competitors and this is an audition for the role of a bitch. Could her kindness have been an attempt to distract me? Nah, she was genuine. And there's no competition here. Nothing we can change at this point, anyway. When it's about a look, either you're what they want or you're not.

When my friend comes out we exchange contact info and say goodbye. As she leaves, the casting director calls the names of the next two contestants: one to audition and another, a petite, frowning woman, to be "on deck." The door to the audition room closes and the frowning woman stands waiting to go in. I wonder if she realizes she's slouching. The power-bitch thing isn't working for her.

"I love your dress," I say, and I mean it. "It really suits you."

She smiles, and with that her shoulders straighten. She puts her hand to the side of her mouth to whisper, "I got it at a resale shop," and we grin. She returns the compliment. "I like your haircut."

We talk briefly about resale and discount stores, and what fun it is to find a bargain. Then the casting director calls her in. She strides into the room: a tough customer, a vicious villain, a tyrant. She can't wait to play the part.

"You're on deck," the casting director tells me. I smile and thank her. I can be nice to her, but I am so ready to be a bitch to that camera.

CHAPTER 24
NOVOCAIN

Like a good little actor, I plan carefully. When the doctor's receptionist is trying to reschedule the appointment I made three months ago, "I have an audition" doesn't placate her any more than "I have a dental appointment" pleases my agent when she's just spent the last half hour on the phone setting it up.

Eighy-thirty in the morning is a good time for the dentist. There's no way that particular appointment can interfere with my professional schedule.

I received the call the evening before my dentist appointment. I had an audition for a national commercial at 10:20 the following morning. No problem.

I got up early, put on a business suit and traipsed off to the dentist for...

(Dah dah dah DAH!) A ROOT CANAL.

It sounds bad, but it's a piece of cake because we have...

(Dah dah dah DAH!) NOVOCAIN!

The doctor numbed me, did his nasty work and was finished by 9:30. See how well this works?

"I hamm an oohnisshion," I told him. He did a double-take. (Dah dah dah DAH!)

We stared at each other in horror. He tried to smile but his expression was pained. "Good luck," he said.

"It's mott 'gud yuck,'" I said. "It's 'mreek a yegg!'"

Bad. Very bad. In desperation, I called my commercial agent, Julie. I'm a good little client. I show up on time and I behave. I rarely ask for favors.

"Hi, Ngoolee. I had moomoocain. Noo you fing me can reshedjal my oohnisshion?"

I was lucky she didn't hang up on me. When she finally figured out who I was and what I wanted she was a little miffed. Who could blame her? Why hadn't I booked out? But she put me on hold and made a call. The latest I could audition was 12:50 p.m.

I had three hours. Whew! The Novocain would wear off by then. I ran errands, keeping to myself so as not to frighten anyone who saw my strangely frozen jaw. I patted my face, thinking for some reason it would help. All morning the thought haunted me that I had not been a good little actor and Julie would be unhappy with me.

Finally, I drove to Hollywood and parked around the corner from the casting office. It was 12:30. In the lighted mirror on my visor my lips looked swollen and twisted, like Angelina Jolie smelled something rancid. I rubbed my cheeks vigorously. I read a magazine article. I plucked my eyebrows.

At 12:45, defeated and still facially paralyzed, I drove away, remembering that my theatrical agent, Blanche, had once said I was reliable, or trustworthy, or...*conscientious*.

I pulled over and called Julie. "Mutt shoon I noo?" I wailed.

"Drive back. Stop in and say hi. Just let them know you tried and you're sorry it didn't work."

I didn't want the casting director to see me all puckered, but I didn't want to disappoint Julie. I drove back, parked, and wobbled to the office on my high heels. It was 1:00. The audition was over. At least that's what I hoped.

But there were still a few actors in the waiting room. Doug, the casting director, spotted me when I entered. "Hi," he said. "We'll take you as soon as you're ready."

The audition wasn't over. I looked at the bulletin board. Tons of copy. All talk.

I smiled at Doug, hoping my grin wasn't too crooked. Then I leaned closer to him and whispered, "I'm yate, an I han Nomakeen."

All faces in the room turned to me. Doug pulled his glasses down his nose and glared. His lips pursed. I was no longer a good little actor.

"Wall, ya shoun fine da me. An ya doon yook too bad. Doeshn't she shoun fine?"

Everyone laughed, forcing me to laugh too, which untwisted my mouth. I was embarrassed but I felt better, having shared my awful secret.

So I auditioned. I even improvised a little, which got a laugh from Doug (apparently casting directors are people, too). My career wasn't over and my agent didn't drop me.

Maybe it wasn't the Novocain that twisted my face. Maybe it was my chagrin. Really, I've got to get over this "good little actor" thing.

◆

CHAPTER 25

SO, THAT HAPPENED

Whee! I'm going to producers for *The Unit*, the searing drama of daring spies, international intrigue and gritty mommies, written and produced by, among others, David Mamet.

David. Mamet.

To a one-time Chicago actor, this is like saying I have a callback for *Titus Andronicus* and William Shakespeare's going to be there.

For me it's especially great because it's a second chance. I auditioned for the show's producers months ago, and I thought I blew it. Mr. Mamet was there, which I hadn't expected, and I did that thing you're not supposed to do: I kind of, well, *gushed*.

It wasn't awful. I was genuinely happy to meet him, and I said, "Oh! Hi!" kind of surprised, and I don't remember which happened first, either he began to stand up or I put out my hand (but it was probably me and he was probably just being nice), and I shouldn't have put out my hand, you're not supposed to do that, there were at least six other people in the room and nobody wants germs and *you're not supposed to shake hands!*

But I did that.

I managed to collect myself and do a decent audition. But I didn't get the job and all this time I've been thinking, "That casting director is never going to call me in again because of my awful (albeit genuine) hand-shaking *faux pas*."

So I'm thrilled to have a second chance, and it just so happens I'm currently reading Mamet's book, *True and False*. Perfect timing! The book is Mamet's take on the actor's job. He says, in a nutshell, it's the writer's job to convey the message of the play, and the actor's job to simply and clearly speak the lines.

That's basically it.

Of course there's more to it but I'm talking nutshell here. Mamet says other things as well, like "nothing in the world is less interesting than an actor on the stage involved in his or her own emotions," and I agree with that. I've seen and even been guilty of some self-indulgent performances that I would have enjoyed missing.

He writes, "*Invent nothing, deny nothing.* This is the meaning of character." Those are his italics, not mine.

Hmm. Invent nothing, deny nothing. Okay. I'll give that a shot for *The Unit*.

With Mamet-sides your pauses are written for you. He tells you where he wants emphasis, and he adds ellipses where he wants you to hesitate, even if it's in the middle of a word. No need to invent those things. It's like doing Shakespeare by the Folio. If you do it as written, you've got the information you need, right? And if you don't do it as written, then you're not doing the script you're given, which is not your job, according to Mamet.

So I work on this piece. I memorize it, emphasizing the underlined words. I pause where the ellipses are. I hes...itate where the script splits a word.

I invent nothing. I deny nothing. I know my objective. That's all I have to do.

So I get there and Mr. Mamet's not there and I do the scene for a camera and two friendly producers with this very nice casting director who has stuck her neck out for me (because when they call an actor directly to producers that's exactly what they're doing) and it goes by quickly and I invent nothing and deny nothing and I say the words the way I rehearsed them and it's over and I step into the hall and I'm wondering what just happened.

Nothing. Nothing happened.

Just saying the lines with an objective in my head wasn't interesting at all.

Whose fault is that? Not David Mamet's.

I gave a bland audition because I concentrated on one thing and neglected pretty much everything else. It was as though I read the lines like a list, and never bothered to put my Self into the role. I don't think that's what Mamet had in mind.

Here's another list, of things I forgot:
1. An objective is not something you think, it's something you play.
2. An actor will have many teachers in her life and will take from each teacher what she can use, so doing *one* thing learned yesterday from *one* teacher's book will likely not be sufficient.

3. I tried to do "what I thought They wanted." No one *ever* knows what They want, not even Them, not until They see it.

4. Once you've rehearsed and prepared, you're not supposed to take your preparation to the audition. You're supposed to throw it away and just do the scene. What I showed them was not a performance. It was a rehearsal.

5. I know what I'm doing, at least when I'm not doubting myself. That's how I got the audition in the first place.

6. Mr. Mamet's book came out in 1999. He might have changed his mind by now.

So you send the casting director a thank you note, you take what you've learned from the experience, and you file it for future use. Then you climb out of the wreckage, say to yourself, "So, that happened," and walk away.

CHAPTER 26
DO-OVER

"Yes, but who needs etiquette when you have…those?" I raised my eyebrows and checked the rearview mirror. Yep. The eyebrow/lip curl combo would get a laugh.

Confident that I was well-prepared, I got out of the car, fed the meter and, with head held high, marched to my first meeting with Ms. Fab, top sitcom casting director.

When I entered her office, Ms. Fab welcomed me with a friendly smile. She was that rare casting director gem, a good acting partner. So why, after all my preparation, did my lines fly out of my mouth like I'd mainlined a gallon of caffeine? That is, until the last line, which tripped off my tongue like a lead ingot. "Yesh, buuut whoooo neeeeeds edikit whennnn yooooo have…thoooze?" I was unable to lift an eyebrow or curl a lip because they were both too damned heavy.

Ms. Fab said "thank you" and I said "thank you," and we both knew that she'd cross me off her list and forget me as soon as I left her office. At least, I hoped she would.

In the quiet reception area, the assistant thanked me for coming in. I glanced at the sign-in sheet. My name was the last one. It was almost noon. Ms. Fab and her assistant would shut the door behind me, order lunch and talk about the actors who had excited them that morning. My name would not be mentioned.

I slouched out the door and down the hall to the exit, smacking my forehead every time I thought of what I should have—could have—done differently! Stuff I did in the shower! Stuff I did in the car! Stuff I would do if only I had a second chance!

I stopped, mid-smack. The second chance was up to me. Could I ask for a do-over? Should I? The scenario was right. It was 11:45, no one was waiting to audition and Ms. Fab was in a good mood.

I turned around and headed back, gaining momentum. I knew how to put my personal spin on that scene and make it fly. I knew how to pace it, where the pauses were, and when to lift those eyebrows.

I also knew the cardinal rule: If you ask for a do-over, you'd better be sure you can **GUARANTEE** a great read the second time around. (I'd add bells and whistles to those bold/underlined/italics/all caps if I could.) And if that do-over isn't granted, say thanks, leave quietly and let it go.

The door was still open. The assistant looked up when I entered. "Forget something?"

I took a breath. "Not exactly." I wasn't sure how to phrase it. "I just thought…I know I can give a better read. If Ms. Fab has the time, may I please try again?"

"I'll check." She picked up the intercom and asked, then smiled up at me. "Go right in."

Ms. Fab could have said no. When I entered her office she could have been intimidating. Instead she said, "I'm delighted to see you again." Her greeting made me feel supercharged. I had never asked for a do-over before, and I'll always be grateful to her for welcoming me back.

Having nothing to lose also helped.

The second time around, I was brilliant! A genius of comedy! I scaled the heights of hilarity! Okay, I didn't waste her time. I delivered the lines with confidence, got her laughing and raised my eyebrows exactly as planned.

I even killed at the callbacks.

You probably want to know if I booked it. Oh, you are so results-oriented! The only reason I didn't book it is that I was funnier than the regulars. Or they wanted to save me for a larger part. Or the show was cancelled. Or not.

Ms. Fab called my agent to say they loved me, she was proud of me, and she'd have me in again.

Not every situation is ripe for a do-over, and repeating what you've already done is a bad move. Even if you can top yourself, if the staff is overrun or behind or wildly bitchy, you have to use your judgment. I trusted my gut in the case of Ms. Fab, and it helped that the situation was right.

The thank you note I sent her was immediate and heartfelt. Good edikit comes in handy.

CHAPTER 27
PRO CHOICE

Paula slogged through 20 miles of gridlock to audition for a commercial. There were two roles for women: the Wife and the Crazy Lady. Paula was called in for the Crazy Lady part. She's a character woman, a comedienne. Perfect.

Like a pro, Paula anticipated the traffic and arrived fifteen minutes before her appointment time. The staff at Miss Thing Casting, however, had not planned well and things were in disarray. Because someone hadn't scheduled properly, the waiting room was packed with Crazy Ladies, with nary a Wife to be found.

It happens.

Miss Thing herself was holed up in the audition room with the client while Assistant Thing was left to her own devices. Desperate, Assistant Thing tried frantically to get organized, which isn't easy in a room full of crazy ladies.

But Paula's not really crazy, she's an actor who knows how to portray a character. Assistant Thing, sensing an ally, asked

Paula to read the Wife role, just to help move the day along.

"Sure," said Paula, feeling her heart sink, because she knew she was better for the Crazy Lady part. But our girl's a team player and Assistant Thing knew a pro when she saw one.

Paula entered the audition room where the director, client and Miss Thing were conversing amid the remnants of lunch. At first they ignored Paula, but finally Miss Thing looked up. She stared. At last she yelled, "YOU cannot be a WIFE!"

The last thing Paula expected was for Miss Thing to yell at her. Usually when you're doing somebody a favor, they treat you more kindly. Paula's first thought was to say—well, that's unprintable—but she's a quick thinker, and instead she said, "Let me call my husband and check with him on that."

Miss Thing didn't think that was funny, nor did she take the opportunity to say, "I'm sorry, I didn't mean to be rude, please read the Crazy Lady." Instead, she continued in her established vein: "YOU'RE TOO OLD!"

Apparently, Miss Thing and Assistant Thing were not on the same page. Right hand lacked a clue as to the method in left hand's madness.

Paula said, "Okay, I got it," and exited the audition room.

At this point some actors might have stayed, in hopes of a chance to read the Crazy Lady role for the crazy lady casting director. But Paula did what I like to think I would have done. She left.

In a situation where you've been treated with disrespect by the client's representative in the client's presence, which is more important to you?

    A) To stay and humiliate yourself in hopes of getting the part? (Is it possible the client might now be predisposed not to work with you? Or...

B) To leave with your self-respect intact? (Is it possible you are now predisposed not to work with this client or this casting director?)

When Paula told me this story I asked her Miss Thing's name. She couldn't remember it. That's because Miss Thing is not important. What's important is Paula's integrity.

In my experience, most people who have the power to hire you are nice. Even if they're not genuinely nice, at least they're professional enough to fake it. The Miss Things of this world are the amateurs.

We all have bad days. Casting directors get overworked like anybody else. But they expect us to hold up under extreme pressure, and we ought to expect the same from them because they're pros, too.

Are you a bratty toddler? Do you require discipline? I doubt it. This isn't kindergarten. It's business. You're a professional. You should be treated like one.

It's going to be a long career. I recommend you establish self-respect early and hold on tight.

CHAPTER 28
RYOKO ROCKS

I am a star.

While I was charging back and forth across Los Angeles trying to get cast in a series, I got cast in one and didn't realize it.

Quite by accident I achieved celebrity status in the niche market of anime, when a friend told me about an audition for *Tenchi Muyo!* I didn't know what that was, but it didn't matter. It was an audition and I went.

What *Tenchi Muyo!* turned out to be was one of the mid-90's anime dubs that together took the youthful American geek population by storm. Producers were just beginning to dub anime from Japanese to English when I got the plum voice-acting role of Ryoko, the sexy space pirate who can walk through walls and fly. (She even has a cabbit, a half-cat/half-rabbit who eats carrots and turns into a spaceship.) Ryoko is madly in love with Tenchi and will fight not only to protect him but to have him for herself. And I do mean fight.

She's a fierce warrior and you'd best not mess with her.

At the time, of course, we had no idea that *Tenchi* would become an anime classic. We recorded lots of episodes and even feature-length films. We enjoyed the work, the cast was wonderful, our producer and director were dreamy and there were snacks. What more can an actor want?

An actor wants to do her best work, that's what. And for the most part, I did. I put my heart and soul into Ryoko. I roared my way through battle scenes, I cooed and coddled Tenchi with my voice, and I growled at the characters Ryoko thought were her competition.

It was all going so well. Then one day the producer told me they needed me to record a rock tune at the next session.

Sing?

Oh no.

"I can't sing," I told her.

"Of course you can sing," she said. "You have a good voice for speaking, so you can sing."

That was very nice of her but it's not the same thing, not the same training. Just because a person speaks well doesn't mean she can sing and vice versa. It's one thing to carry a tune. (I carry a tune like it's a boulder.) It's another thing to *rock*.

But the producer buttered me up and convinced me to give it a shot. She had me believing I could sing a rock and roll song. And why not? All I had to do was belt it out, maybe give it some grind, some heft. I knew how to grind and heft. I could do that!

I went home to practice in the shower. And damn, I was good! How is it that the shower turns us all into Ann Wilson? I belted out that tune 'til the neighbors pounded on the walls, begging me to shut up.

I wasn't as confident at the recording session. The engineer thought I was being temperamental when I made him move the microphone to a spot behind a wall in the booth where no one could see me. I wasn't being temperamental. I was being terrified.

I put on the headphones. We checked the levels. I told them I was ready. I was not. I never would be.

The intro played and out it came, my "singing voice," the one that isn't always on tune or off, the one that has a sort of hitch in its get-along, the one with a B flat that's not really flat, just lazy, the one that no one in their right mind would play in a public forum. That one. Out it came, loud if not clear.

I didn't carry that tune, I dragged it. I hefted it against the wall then ground it under the heel of my shoe. I didn't sound a bit like Ann Wilson. I sounded like the worst *American Idol* audition ever. (Seriously. Search it on YouTube).

At least the producer spared me the humiliation of a second take. She was even kind enough to joke about it: "Maybe you're right, just because a person talks good doesn't mean they sing good. Hahahahaha."

I slumped and sagged all the way home. I felt so low it's a miracle I could see over the steering wheel to drive.

I hadn't done my best work.

But it was the best I could do. I wished I could have done what they wanted me to do but I needed to acknowledge there were—there are—some things of which I'm not capable.

I don't think this one was anyone's fault. Perhaps the producer shouldn't have pushed me so hard to do something I was clearly uncomfortable with. Perhaps I should have been more adamant in my refusal.

In the end it worked out. The producer found someone who could sing the song and sound like the character I'd already voiced in so many episodes. I kept the job. Plus I got to talk-sing for the karaoke episode, and that one's a comedy classic.

After nearly 20 years, people still love *Tenchi Muyo!* Its success sneaked up on me. Being part of it, even as a very bad singer, was a most fortunate accident.

CHAPTER 29
BLESSING-COUNTING TIME

- Headshots printed: check.
- Résumés updated, printed, and trimmed to 8X10 size: check.
- The above attached to each other and delivered to agent: check.
- All of the above on the web, along with current, snappy videos: check.
- Audition clothes, dating from this century, back from the dry cleaners: check.
- Non-denominational semi-politically correct holiday cards mailed: check.
- New Year's resolutions made: check.
- Goals for next year listed, itemized, broken into teeny, tiny, anal-retentive baby steps and marked on calendar: check.

That's everything. I'm ready for the New Year.

So what's an actor to do with herself while all of Hollywood is on vacation?

Well, maybe nothing.

Actors work hard all year. Even when we're not Working, we work. We take a class, rehearse a play, send a mailing, self-promote. We're always at the work's beck and call. We drop everything to race to an audition at the last minute, miles away, in rush hour, without the slightest guarantee of compensation. Call us and we'll do everything we can to show up, with no promise of pay, not even a "maybe." We'll bust our butts for a "probably not."

We go, gladly, again and again. We throw our hearts, souls, minds and bodies into our work because we love it.

But it's okay to take a break, and the holidays can be a good time to kick back. Most casting offices are closed until mid-January, so you can even leave town without taking a chance you'll miss out on anything. And you can always make it back if you need to.

There's something to be said for not obsessing about work for a while, and instead taking time to be with people you love. Those same people have probably been supportive of your career all year long. Regardless of one's religious persuasion or lack thereof, there's renewal in communion: with others, with nature, with ancestors, with ritual. Our very craft grew from the primeval ritual of storytelling.

I find it's a good time of year for gazing (or howling) at the moon, catching up on projects or reading, and taking extended wilderness hikes with Socrates, my husband, and Phiz, our canine kin. We have our phones but nobody calls. Unlike other times of year it's fine for the phone not to ring.

I bundle up. I'm from the Midwest but I've acclimated to southern California, so when it gets below 70 degrees I need layers. Socrates deigns to wear a flannel shirt over his tee.

Local trails, blanketed with leaves (our winter equivalent of snow), make a good adventure of smells for Phiz. We've got a couple of apples, a bottle of water, and the clouds.

There's one task left for me to complete before we head out: it's blessing-counting time.

- A safe, warm home to return to: check.
- Food in the fridge: check.
- Enough money to pay the bills: check.
- Our work to pursue in the new year: check.
- Friends and family: check.
- Each other: check.

Whatever holidays or traditions you celebrate, may they be sweet, and filled with more blessings than you can count.

CHAPTER 30
'TIS THE SEASON

Our business has seasons, and some are less brisk than others. December can be downright dull, if what you crave is paying work. But pilot season's a'comin' and you'd better be ready!

It's a frenzied time! Take advantage of the lull over the holidays because it's about to get *crrrazy-busy* in January! Are your headshots current? Do your audition clothes still fit? Is your phone bill paid? Are your business cards printed? Manicure done? Passport up-to-date? Nose blown? Did everybody go to the bathroom? Because we're not stopping for a break 'til March!

Everyone gets worked up about pilot season. I've read interviews with casting directors who talk about how hectic it is for them as well as for actors, how they're reading scripts and responding to demands from producers and directors, and how their hearts go out to actors because we're going to three or more pilot auditions a day.

Excuse me? Three or more pilot auditions *a day?*

My life should suck that much.

Am I the only one for whom pilot season can be the slowest time of year? Is everybody else studying their sides late into the night, schlepping an entire wardrobe in the car, living on coffee and granola bars and changing clothes while changing lanes? Could I be the only one who waits for pilot season to end so I can start working again?

Just as Hollywood goes through its production seasons, actors go through career ups and downs. I shouldn't admit this, but I've had pilot seasons that rival the week between Christmas and New Year's for lack of auditions. Sometimes you're hot and sometimes you're not and right now, I'm tepid.

It's not that I've never auditioned for a pilot. I've auditioned for plenty of pilots, I'll have you know. But they haven't been pilot auditions *per se* because they weren't for contract roles. Instead, I've auditioned for small roles *in the pilot episode*: the clerk at the newsstand where the star buys his paper, the desk cop the star flirts with for a few seconds, the receptionist the star needs to get past to see the other star.

Maybe this will be my year. In my heart of hearts, I'm holding out hope for that pilot season where I'm the busy one—where every new series cries out for someone like me: a kind of funny, not bad-looking professional type who is, let's face it, incredibly sexy. I just hope it happens soon or I'll be waiting for the pilot season where every show stars a doddering, elderly, (still incredibly sexy but) bitter old woman.

I would like at least one pilot season that isn't as slow as the holidays. You know, one where I have, oh, maybe three auditions a week (imagine!), and a reason to get a manicure.

CHAPTER 31

AGEISM

If 50 is the new 30, then why are thirty-something female stars scrambling for appointments with the plastic surgeon? Why are handsome young men getting hair plugs and destroying their birth records? Why do screenwriters in their forties refuse to meet producers face to face?

Because they don't want the money guys to know how old they are.

It's as though we're living the nightmare of *Soylent Green*. (Look it up. Or admit you're old enough to remember.)

I've decided not to worry about age. Worrying gives me age lines and I already have enough. Plus, the plastic surgery route isn't for me.

I started getting the occasional gray hair when I was in my twenties. I dyed my hair for a long time. In fact I'd forgotten what color it was until my husband suggested I just, you know, see.

Well surprise, surprise, my hair's grey. Most of it, anyway.

There's still some—I don't know what you call it, not brown, not blonde, maybe beige? Still some of that mixed in. You could call my color "salt and coriander."

As soon as I stopped dying my hair the strangest thing happened: I started working more. Oh sure, you say, it's a humor column. But I'm not kidding.

I wondered if it was because I was letting my age show, so I tried something else. I wore my glasses to auditions. At first I was afraid it would hurt my chances, but with glasses I could actually see the copy.

What a breakthrough!

It turns out casting directors, directors, writers, producers and pretty much everybody likes it when you can read the copy. Some of them even like glasses, and they want you to wear them on TV! I kid you not. Next I'm going to try hobbling, see where that gets me.

I'd rather put my best foot forward, though, bunions and all. I can't do better than being myself and there are variations on that, good and bad. I admit I obsess about my age sometimes. It's hard not to worry about it in our business. I glance around my yoga class, wistfully comparing myself to younger women (or, maliciously, to older ones). But at least I'm in yoga class.

I've been reading an old copy of *Who Moved My Cheese?* in my agent's bathroom, midway between Warner Brothers and Sunset/Gower. Simply put, the book is a warning: don't stagnate. Keep up with your business, whatever it is, and move forward with the trends. Embrace change.

So for all of us actors who are, shall we say, *beyond* hottie, here's a "Who Moved My Cheesecake/Beefcake?" checklist to keep us on our toes:

1. Body

How's your instrument? Fabulous? Fat? Funky? Make sure you look and smell like someone with whom others can stand to work. And take care of your health. No one wants to hire you if they're afraid you're going to keel over on the set.

2. Soul

Are you a positive person? Are you easy to accommodate, or do you complain about the lack of gluten-free snacks on the craft services table? Do you tell the director how to direct?

3. Brain

Can you still memorize? What do you do to keep your wits sharp? Take naps? Spend the day on Facebook?

4. Business

Acting has changed since the 1980's, since the 1990's, since 2013, for that matter. Have you taken a class in the last two years? Five years? Ten? Are your headshots up-to-date? Is there an 8x10 black & white glossy of you with wide lapels, a dickey and a comb-over still floating around the casting offices of Hollywood? Which brings up the question: Does your headshot look like you look today, or like you looked when Bill Clinton was president? (If you don't remember him, you can stop reading now.)

5. Technology

Most important: are you online? If you're not online and networking, you're not in business.

We can do a lot to make ourselves viable as actors in the 21st century. Beyond that we can play only the roles we're right for, and that's true no matter your age. Much as I hate to admit it I'm too old to play opposite Channing Tatum or Brad Pitt. Hell, in this business I'm too old to play opposite Clint Eastwood. But I am who I am. If that's in the breakdown, I'll get the job because no one can play it better.

CHAPTER 32

I AM THE HOT FLASH!

The subject of menopause was taboo for my mother's generation. Even now medical science knows next to nothing about it. But I've had it, I tell you, and I'm coming out of the menopausal closet because frankly, it's too hot in here.

They told me my body would change as I got older. They told me my bones would get creaky, my hair would turn gray and I'd have to exercise more to stay slim. I'm not crazy about these things, but at least I expected them. However, when they said my body was an instrument, I wasn't prepared for my Stradivarius to become a butt trumpet.

How does this relate to acting, you may ask?

Look, some of us don't work every day and we're already nervous just navigating the studio environment. We have enough to concentrate on without the added burden of rampaging hormones. Didn't we just get line changes and don't we have to hit our mark and isn't the star in a tizzy and doesn't the crew want to go home and isn't everything riding on this very shot? Isn't that enough? Must we add hot flashes and flatulence to the mix?

No amount of Beano could prevail against the volumes of soy I'm ingesting. I'd skip the soy, but it's the only thing between me and "mood swings," a charming euphemism I like to use for "suicidal depression" and "howling fits of spittle-flecked rage." Flatulence is the lesser of evils. And I do mean evil, and not that much lesser.

And new symptoms continue to appear, like car after car on an endless, runaway freight train. My latest: muscle spasms. You know. Little, tiny tics. In my face.

Here's how panic feels: you work only every couple of months. You're on the set. It's been a long day and finally the camera is on you. Mr. DeMille is ready to shoot your close-up. You're hot, beet red and sweating. It's too bad about the wardrobe, that's already ruined. But damn it, you know your lines and you refuse, *refuse* to let your concentration be ruined by gut-wrenching gas pains and big, manly farts.

Then your eye begins to twitch.

"Action!"

Oh! Oh no, no, no! Stop twitching! Can they see it? Will it show up in post? Will the take be ruined? Will I be fired? Is my career over? Do I have nerve damage? What's happening to me? Maybe if I turn my head a little bit...

"Cut! What's wrong? Just say the line, sweetheart. No pause. And, uh, do it without that blinking thing, okay? Okay. Back to ones!"

But I can't control it. I don't know how.

Muscle spasms, what fun! Turns out this, too, is a symptom of menopause. What *isn't* a symptom of menopause? Acid reflux? Texting while driving? Global warming?

When I was eleven, my mother told me about menstruation. She said it was beautiful and womanly. When my first period arrived I remember thinking, "Somebody lied. This may be womanly but I'm not seeing the beauty here." I'm not going to lie to you younger women about the polar reversal you're going to experience in a few years. By the time you get here, I hope modern medical science is a little more, oh, *modern*. Right now, you're on your own. Doctors shrug and say, "Have you tried black magic—eh, cohosh?"

NOBODY KNOWS ANYTHING.

They don't even know which symptoms are menopausal and which ones are just your cute, personal, girlie quirks. You may emit odd noises or experience spasms, for example. There may be temporary memory loss. If I drop a line or lose the car or forget my husband's name, I blame it on The Change.

Hormones run just about every function of your body, so I'm saying it's estrogen's fault that my jeans are so tight they're painful, that we have only olives in the fridge, that the wallpaper in the kitchen is so ugly, and that although yesterday I was in a perfectly good mood, today both my husband and my dog are avoiding me.

That could also be due to the butt trumpet. Either way, it's not my fault.

CHAPTER 33
MY LUCKY BREAK

"Dans les champs de l'observation le hasard ne favorise que les esprits préparés." Or…

"In the fields of observation, chance favors only the prepared spirits." Or…

"Chance favors the prepared mind."

Louis Pasteur said that and I like to repeat him. He meant if you've done the work, when your lucky break comes, you won't blow it. You'd think old Lou was an actor instead of a scientist.

Are you waiting for your lucky break, the magical key that opens your door to the big-time? Where's it gonna come from? Who's gonna give it to you? Who do I have to sleep with around here to be a star?

I've finally figured it out. I don't have to sleep with anybody! (That can be good or bad, depending on who's doing the sleeping.) All I have to do to get my lucky break is prepare for it. We don't always recognize luck, but it happens all the time.

I recently met a lady named Susan who told me the story of her lucky break. She'd decided not to study acting and instead worked as an extra while waiting for her break to come. She thought being on the set would give her opportunities to perform. She was right.

One day, an actor was late to the shoot. The director couldn't wait because time is money, baby! He needed someone right away to play the missing actor's part. He thought Susan looked right and handed her a script.

She couldn't do it. She was too terrified. She had never actually acted and she didn't know what was expected of her. She was so nervous her voice shook.

There it was, her lucky break, handed to her on a silver platter. And she wasn't ready to receive it.

If the director had handed, oh, say, an unknown Jennifer Lawrence that script, do you think she would have stepped up to the plate?

Opportunity knocks all the time. What separates the star from the wannabe is not just opening the door and inviting it in. It's having snacks and beverages on hand. Not just beer and chips, either, but mixed drinks and fancy hors d'oeuvres.

Such as shrimp cocktail. I like shrimp cocktail.

I'm glad I figured this out because it's good news. Lucky breaks are everywhere! All I have to do is prepare.

…And prepare and prepare, not just in the overall sense of taking classes and keeping up my chops, but also in the smaller sense of each individual audition.

I don't know about you, but I memorize my sides. I memorize so that if the Susan part of me shows up I'm ready for her. I carry the script at the audition so Susan can look at it if she needs to. But the Jennifer part of me is prepared. She has worked on the sides until she knows them inside and out, then she's worked on them some more. Susan can freak out all she wants to, because Jennifer is in charge and she carries the day. This way, the only trouble I have is splitting the paychecks between the three of us and still having enough to pay the shrink.

Preparing also means gathering information: checking the show's web presence, learning about its actors, directors and producers, watching the show for style, and reading anything I can find about the casting director's quirks and preferences. If it's for a film, I check IMDb to learn about the people involved. To quote a great philosopher (my husband, Socrates), "There's no such thing as too much information."

Deborah Kerr said, "The 'being discovered at the soda fountain' routine is the rare exception which proves the rule. The thing to be is prepared. Finding yourself on top without being prepared will pull you down faster than you got up there." Ms. Kerr was in a position to know.

Luck is ubiquitous. Every audition is a lucky break. Each job is, too. And no one's perfect. There are days when I prepare for my lucky break by sitting on my butt and surfing the web. But then I remember Jennifer, and I click on the acting sites or move my butt to yoga class. I may never end up with a silver platter, but when opportunity knocks, I will at least have shrimp cocktail to serve it, and maybe even champagne.

◆

CHAPTER 34

HOW I SPENT MY SUMMER VACATION

Hunky Norman took a vacation. Hunky Norman is Blanche's hot young assistant. As you may recall, Blanche is my agent and long-time friend. Sometimes I fill in at her office when she needs an extra hand. It keeps me current on the world of headshots, agents, casting directors and doofuses.

I've spent an afternoon here and there helping Blanche with the phones but this time I worked nearly three weeks, long enough to get my nose rubbed in the incessant realities of Blanche's world, that of a growing Los Angeles talent agency. I learned thousands of painful truths.

One of my duties was opening the mail. Even at Blanche's small shop there are mounds of it every day. I can't imagine the insanity the assistants endure at William Morris. They must have to go through the mail with shovels.

Pawing through the daily avalanche, I learned there's no way to guarantee an agent will call you in from your submission. You can't be certain you'll fit their needs. However, there are ways to guarantee you *won't* be called in. Here are some of my favorites, all of which I already knew and I bet you know them, too, because you are a pro:

1. Some people send in weird, arty photos. They cover their faces with their hands or wear wild make-up, or cloak their eyes in shadow for a bit of mystery. They let the photographer blend their body or hair into the background, blurring shape and texture. They crop their photos at the top (Blanche assumes this means they're bald). They use ephemeral lighting so it's about the photographer's style and not what the actor looks like. A few die-hards still send those charming, retro, black-and-white glossies. On a computer screen, a black-and-white photo has a subtle way of fading into the background when placed alongside the snappy, color headshots of the competition. Some folks try to save money. One person blew up a snapshot and sent it in. She looked startled. That wasn't me. And it wasn't you.

2. Some people don't include a note with their submission. That's a sure-fire way to get sent to the recycle bin. Even small agencies have more than one department (theatrical, commercial, print, sports, children, etc.). You and I know to mention what we're submitting *for*.

3. We're pros, you and I, so we print our contact information on our résumés, and we add it to our cover letters along with a notation of union status. We include our phone number, website and email address. Amateurs mark themselves clearly by not marking themselves clearly.

4. There are those who include the letter, clearly stating contact information, experience and intentions, and

leave out the headshot. It's not an oversight. The letter is folded deliberately and mailed in a #10 business envelope. It's a novel approach, don't you think? Come on, an agent doesn't need to know what an actor looks like. I mean, really, this business is way too concerned with appearances.

5. You and I would never do this, but some people insult their previous agent in their cover letters, forgetting that even though it's a big town it's a small world, and they might be slamming a colleague of the agent they're attempting to impress.

6. Some amateurs lie on their résumés. It goes without saying that professionals don't have to do this, even professionals with very few credits. Professionalism isn't about what you've done but about the integrity you've put into it.

7. One thing professionals know to do is research. We find out if an agent is open to receiving submissions, and before we submit we know what type of talent the agency represents. I won't be submitting to a sports agency, for example. And although amateurs might think agents are not people and don't need to be treated as such, professionals know better and would never address a letter to "Dear Agent" or to "To Whom It May Concern."

8. My favorite: A pro would never do this, but an amateur might walk into a busy agency and just ask for representation. He might do this between late morning and early afternoon during the rush to get submissions out to the casting offices. He might get good and stoned to get his courage up and he might even prepare some jokes, or

imitations, or a soft-shoe to perform in the lobby while watching the assistants frantically answering phones and stuffing submission envelopes.

You and I would never do that.

And that was just the first day. After a couple of weeks on the other side of the desk I really missed Hunky Norman, and I came to understand why agents sometimes roll their eyes when they talk about actors. They're not talking about you. They're talking about the thousands of amateurs who flood the business.

Unfortunately, those well-meaning-but-clueless wannabees have as much right to submit as you and I do, which means the agencies have to dig through a mountain of what amounts to trash in order to find your submission.

The competition is fierce. The best way to stand out from the crowd is to be your finest, most professional self. There's no need to be wacky or weird, unless that's your nature. When your submission shows up with a straightforward note, an honest résumé and a well-done headshot that looks like an actual human (you), it's the exception. If you're the exception that fills the agency's need, you're in. That part—the agency's need—is out of your control.

CHAPTER 35

CHANNEL SURFING

Every New Year I resolve to land a regular role in a TV series, win an Academy Award and lose ten pounds. This year I've been trying to come up with a resolution that's actually within my power.

Well, did I ever have an "aha" moment in the frozen foods aisle at the grocery store! I was thinking about my extra ten pounds vs. vanilla chocolate chip ice cream when I thought, why work so hard?

It's obvious. I'm going to learn how to channel.

Wikipedia defines channeling as "the esoteric process of receiving messages or inspiration from extra-dimensional beings or spirits, whereby one is a medium or channel for such an entity."

How hard can that be? It stands to reason that you or I could be a medium to channel one of these "entities." Entities can be indeterminate spiritual guides or they can be specific people from the past. Specific dead people.

Channeling is the obvious choice if you're playing a historic figure. Can you achieve greater precision than actually being the person you're portraying? Even when playing fictional characters, it makes sense to channel. I don't know why more actors don't do it.

Think of the possibilities. If you're a gentle soul and you find it difficult to play someone vicious, why not just conjure Caligula? Uncomfortable with your sexuality? Muster up Marilyn Monroe. It's so much simpler than dredging up all that drama in yourself.

Acting classes have been known to become mini-therapy sessions, and some actors aren't ready to reveal their souls to teachers or fellow students, much less the viewing public. I say skip the acting classes. Learn how to channel and let the entity do the revealing. When you come out of your trance, everyone will think you're amazing.

"It won't work," you say, or "There's more to acting than just being the role." I've thought of that. You must channel someone intelligent enough to learn their lines and blocking. I grant you this rules out a few alleged geniuses, such as Joseph Stalin, Kim Jong Il and Queen "Bloody" Mary I.

Better yet, channel a better actor. Why bother to go through the years of training it takes to become as brilliant an actor as, say, Peggy Ashcroft, when you can channel Ms. Peggy herself? Just remember to channel someone deceased. You may admire Christian Bale, but it's likely he's busy and I don't recommend messing with him. And hurry up and pick somebody or all the good ones are going to be taken.

I must caution you: there are dangers. You're giving over control, so before you dive in, consider the possibilities and be prepared. Here are a few pointers (By now it's clear I like lists):

1. *Do your research.*
You want to know exactly who your historical figure is before you invite his or her ectoplasm into your didies.

2. *Channel someone clean.*
Don't bring odors or itching problems to the set. Channeling an 18th century French bureaucrat, for example, might not be a good idea unless you're willing to channel him at home first and give him a shower.

3. *Channel someone willing.*
Just because Vlad Dracul is perfect for the part doesn't mean he's going to behave.

4. *Channel at the right moment*
Sarah Siddons doesn't know how to drive herself to an audition, so wait until you get there and channel her in the ladies' room.

5. *Get your real vs. fictional people straight.*
Lancelot du Lac isn't going to show up to play Lancelot du Lac.

6. *Know how to send your entity home*
You don't want to be sharing that paycheck. The point is to make the money without having to do the work. Plus, what if you *did* channel Caligula? If you can't get rid of him, the grocery bills are going to be monumental. Not to mention the tab for penicillin.

Which returns me to the grocery store, the ice cream aisle, and those ten pounds. I wonder if Mata Hari likes soy?

CHAPTER 36
THE KINDEST CUT

From: Vivvy
To: Undisclosed Recipients

Tune in your DVR December 16th! I've got a nice part on Lives of Inconsequence! Love to all...

I like to see my friends on TV, so I marked my calendar and watched. Vivvy walked across the screen. Once.

One doesn't generally send a mass email about background work, but okay.

A few days later:

From: Vivvy
To: Petrea

The one time I let everyone know I was on TV, I was cut! Has it happened to you? I'd love to know your coping skills. Do you put out the word when you know you can be edited? Of course I sent a mailing to casting directors. How does one handle the embarrassment?

From: Petrea
To: Vivvy

Yes, it's happened to me and I'm still bitter! (Speaking of coping skills.) Comfort yourself that casting directors don't schedule their TV watching around mailings from actors. If they're interested, they'll keep your post card as a reminder to call you in. I've been called in from my post card three times and cast once. In none of these cases did the CD see the show I was publicizing. So keep sending post cards. Casting directors like them and it tells them you're working.

Surely Kevin Costner was heartbroken when Lawrence Kasdan cut him from *The Big Chill*. Some say Kasdan promised Kevin a part in his next movie as consolation. Maybe Kasdan just remembered Costner. Either way, that next movie turned out to be *Silverado*, Kevin's big break.

It's no shame to be cut. It happens to everyone. To some of us it happens twice. So far.

The first time, Socrates and I were moving during the week of the shoot. I had booked out for moving day and the production company assured my agent it wouldn't be a problem. So I accepted the job—a meaty scene on a low-budget cable drama.

When the assistant director phoned the night before my move with an early call time the next morning, I was stuck. Can one say "I can't work tomorrow, I'm booked out"? Sure, and never work in this town again. It's just not possible to reschedule a shoot, not to mention a moving van, at 10:00 the night before. My darling husband Socrates would have to manage the move on his own.

Everyone in the production office felt bad about the mix-up. Through my agent, it was agreed my scene would be shot first so I could get home and prevent Socrates from leaving behind my antique dishes (the ones he doesn't like). I thought that was more than fair.

Apparently no one bothered to explain things to the show's star. I met her in Hair & Makeup where she was having her famous bangs fluffed, and she seemed as sweet as she looked. But as soon as I stepped outside she shouted to the make-up person, "Who the #^@& is she? Why are we shooting her first? She's a #^@&ing nobody!" Et cetera. And the noise continued.

I'm hard pressed to remember her name at the moment. I have worked with bigger stars, before and since, and never have I seen such a tantrum or heard such language on the set. Not even from the Teamsters.

Thankfully my scenes were not with Bangs. But once the shouting died down the set wasn't exactly friendly. At the time it was the biggest TV part I'd ever had and I wanted to give it my all. But the director was in a hurry to get my scene over with. The sooner they got me out of there the happier Bangs would be, and the terrified Teamsters could come out of hiding. I got one take of each shot, and that was it.

At least the move went well. I still have those ugly dishes to prove it. Once Socrates and I were in our new home I moved aside the boxes, found my desk and ordered post cards. I sent one to every casting director in town with a personal note, telling them about my appearance on the show. I called or emailed everyone I could think of. I told my neighbors, new and old. I told the grocery clerk, the guy at the dry cleaner's and everyone at the dog park. I publicized that two-bit show like mad.

You already know they cut me.

Without my scene, the plot didn't even make sense. If

they'd sacrifice plot logic to cut me, I must have been awful!

But...wouldn't the director have, you know, *directed* me if he'd wanted me to do something else?

Maybe in the rush they missed a continuity problem, or they were using film but forgot to put it in the camera, or I had a booger they couldn't digitize out. (Who knew boogers were analog?) Maybe they didn't give a damn about plot logic and cut the scene for commercials. Or maybe, just maybe, they cut me to satisfy Bangs.

Nah. There's too much money riding on these shows to cut an actor for personal reasons. (One would hope.) And besides, it's useless to second-guess these things. One has to let it go.

Regardless, it would have been nice if someone had called to let me know. That small kindness would have saved me a few hundred dollars in printing and postage, not to mention a lot of humiliation. Plus it hurts to be cut. It just plain hurts.

The second time I was cut I had one tiny line on a big-budget, number one network drama. Everyone on the set welcomed me. The director needed real tears from me, and took time to guide me gently through my short scene. When my work was finished, he actually thanked me for appearing on his show.

When they realized my scene didn't advance the plot, the casting director called my agent to tell her I was cut. She said they liked my work so being cut was good, because it made me available for a larger role.

One little phone call from this busy woman almost made being cut a pleasure.

Okay, not. But it was no shame.

It might have been difficult for Kasdan to make that call

to Costner, but surely it was more difficult for Costner to receive it. And Kasdan had the class to make it.

Sometimes we work with the Kasdans. Sometimes we work with the GetThisOverWiths. When you invest in a mailing, the casting director who receives your card doesn't know you were cut; he or she only knows you're working. And your friends, the real ones, will forgive you anything.

From: Vivvy
To: Petrea

BTW, I got some beautiful emails. A high school friend commented that in my case the camera makes you lose 10 lbs! Another friend wrote "love the curls!" My favorite was from an actress who said "I bet they have a bigger part they'd rather use you for." (I entertain the hope she could be right.) One guy said, "Way to walk across a room!"

On the days I think about how hard it is to book the jobs, it's nice to know that true friends will support our efforts during the times we forget to acknowledge how fortunate we are to be living our dreams. Most people wish to be on TV and we go the extra step to make it happen.

Maybe that's it, Vivvy. Sometimes the extra step feels like a step backward. But I think I hear you saying it's worth it.

CHAPTER 37
EN GARDE!

Once upon a time, a beautiful young actress imagined bad things that never happened. The Ogre of Fear ruled her, sending awful scenarios through her head and blocking her entrance to the castle.

When she asked for extra lunch-hour time for an audition, in her mind she'd have to fight with the ruthless boss at her day job. On the way to the audition she'd imagine a new scenario: a defensive rap with the ugly step-casting assistant about the horrid traffic, the dearth of parking spaces or the cruel day job boss who had made the beautiful actress late.

Okay, it wasn't a beautiful young actress. It was a fortyish, kind of tired actress. I imagined things, replaying old stories in new situations where they didn't belong. I had a great boss at my day job who supported me so fully that she not only let me take time for auditions, once she even drove me to one and waited, parked on the mean streets of Hollywood, hunkered down in her shiny Jeep with all the doors locked.

And when I've been late to auditions, the casting people have always been gracious and are almost never ugly.

I was afraid to ask for audition time, afraid I'd get lost on the way, afraid I'd be late, afraid people wouldn't approve of me. Afraid, afraid, afraid. But fear was a fairy tale I brought from an earlier life. In real life, people are generally supportive. If there's an occasional imperfection, they're willing to give me the benefit of the doubt.

Once I grokked this I conquered the Ogre of Fear, forcing him to take refuge in his lair. But he wasn't dead. He waited for a weakness, when I went through another pilot season without a pilot audition.

Except one.

And it wasn't for a series regular.

And I didn't get it.

Then, on Friday before the Monday shoot, my agent called. They wanted to hire me. Not for the role I'd auditioned for, but for a smaller part. A one-liner.

Now before you tell me I should be grateful: first, I know that. Second, this was my seventeenth pilot season in Los Angeles. Third, I've played some of Shakespeare's greatest roles. (Yeah, well, haven't we all?) I wanted to turn down the job but I have bills to pay.

The production office didn't send me a script. Instead, the assistant director called and gave me my line over the phone: two words. We joked that I'd spend the weekend working on it. I tried to do my usual prep but my heart wasn't in it. I didn't know who the principal actors were. I knew of the director and I wanted to do well so he'd hire me again. But how do you show your stuff in two words?

Monday it rained. Poured. Traffic was horrible. The rain

provided a curtain to hide the drama in my car. Once upon a time, imaginary arguments had taken place in my head, but that day my car was crowded with nonexistent people, shouting out my fears at the top of their lungs.

The assistant director yelled from the back seat, "You're late! You were called for 7 o'clock!"

I snapped back, "Do you see this rain? Back off!"

The script supervisor popped up next to the A.D., blocking my rearview mirror. "Didn't anyone call you? They've cut your line. You're an extra."

I yelled, "Oh yeah? Then I'm outta here!"

The star, some new-in-town hotshot I'd never heard of, sat in the passenger seat and refused to speak to me at all. He thought I was a nobody because I had a two-word line and there's gray in my hair.

"And who are *you*?" I said. "*Who* thinks I'm nobody?"

Who indeed? There was no one in my car but me and one, big monster. The Ogre of Fear had escaped his lair.

I exited the freeway and pulled over on a side street. You can't drive and fight monsters at the same time. I was going to be a couple of minutes late, but I had an Ogre to conquer.

The trouble with fear is that it can lead to bad behavior, which is unseemly in beautiful young actors, even if they have gray hair. Frightened people get defensive, sullen, snobbish. Bad behavior is a measure of how terrified a person is. Remember that the next time you see it. It might help you to understand.

The rain pounded on the roof of my car. I drew my sword.

I reminded myself I'm a working actor, and being a working actor sometimes requires just that: working. Just the day-to-day, one line parts. The actor who leaps directly to stardom is the rarity. Baby steps are the norm.

Some days the steps are just really, really tiny. I mean, not even a damned inch. *And I might never get there.*

Whoops. That was the Ogre, getting in his jab.

I parried him: each baby step is an opportunity if I make it so. If I said my two words well enough, if I was friendly and efficient enough, if I enhanced the production instead of being a drag on it, I could work with those people again. If I didn't, I couldn't.

Pollyanna, said the Ogre, baring his pointy teeth.

And thrust: I didn't know who "those people" were going to be, so I decided they'd be perfectly nice folks who'd be glad to see me. In turn, I would be delighted to see them and spend a day working on their show. It was done. I decreed it.

The Ogre didn't die. He's too big to kill in five minutes. But I wounded him. He hopped out of the car and lumbered off into a ditch along the roadside, impervious to the rain that soaked his stinky fur. I'll probably have to fight him again but I was running late.

I took a deep breath, shoved my bloody sword under the seat and rode—uh, drove—off into the rain, with the windshield wipers making nice clippitty-clop hoof-beat sounds.

The sentry at the studio gate was friendly, despite the downpour. The assistant director, a fair maiden who'd been watching for me, met me at my car with an umbrella and a smile. I smiled back. Beyond her the sound stage stood like a castle in the rain. For that day I was perhaps not royalty, but I was at least a member of the court.

CHAPTER 38

POLLYANNA'S LAMENT

Lately I can't seem to do anything at auditions except suck. I guess you'd call it a slump.

People have accused me of being a Pollyanna because I'm an optimist, but these days I can't fool myself. My auditions have been awful. Not so awful that I fall on my face or spit on someone or embarrass myself in spectacular ways. In my nightmare, several casting directors are sitting around and one says "the worst audition I ever saw was Petrea Bur—" and before she can finish her sentence another CD says "She's the worst I ever saw, too!" and pretty soon they're all shouting, "Us, too! She was so bad we had to air out the room after she left!"

But the reality is worse than that. My auditions have been so dull, so utterly forgettable, that no one will ever remember me from them.

Everything seems normal. I get the sides. I learn the script, study the beats, try different reads until I find something interesting to do with the role. I plan what to wear. I know the route and the parking situation. I prepare.

On audition day everything's smooth. There's nothing different going on. I'm in a good mood. I have my coffee and granola, and I check my email. I play with Phiz, the sweetest, coolest dog in the world. I kiss Socrates, the sweetest, coolest husband in the world.

I have nothing to complain about.

Life's great. As a matter of fact, I'm ready. I *own* this part. I know exactly what I'm going to do in the audition and *I can't lose!*

Doo de doo de doo. Cruise along the freeway, park the car, check the mirror for anything gross the toothbrush might have missed, enter the casting office with good posture and a smile. They call my name and I feel fine. I enter the room, say hello, the casting director begins to read and POOF! I disappear.

Why does this happen?

If I knew the answer, I wouldn't be sitting here kicking myself.

It's like a fog comes between me and my intentions as soon as the casting director begins to speak. My personality goes missing—my sense of humor, my confidence, my *me*. We need those things, don't we? Without them auditions become miserable, empty experiences.

We all know how to act, but auditioning is a different animal. I've had hot streaks—times when I thought, "I get it! All I have to do is remember *this feeling* and put my brain *here* for each audition." Lately, though, the feeling flits away like lint on a breeze, and I forget what it was. What if I never find it again? What if I have no control over it? What if it comes and goes on its own with no explanation whatsoever, like popularity or a migraine?

Lately I think I'm confusing the casting directors. *What is she doing here? How did she ever get any credits on her resume? There must be a mistake, this can't be the actress we called in.* When I finish reading, I perceive a tiny moment when the casting director and I look at each other, both of us disappointed, before she (very generously) says "thank you." I leave with my tail between my legs, feeling like I've wasted everyone's time. It's all I can do to get to the car before the tears roll.

But I told you I'm an optimist. I'm allowed to feel sorry for myself only for so long. Then I have to move on. I remind myself, for example, that at least I have a car to cry in. Yeah, gas is almost $5.00 a gallon but hey—I have $5.00. I can go home because I have a home, I know where it is, and Socrates and Phiz are there.

I've auditioned well before and I'll audition well again, or at least that's what Pollyanna tells me. Slumps happen to everyone and this, too, shall pass.

Today I had no auditions. Socrates, Phiz and I went for a hike in the mountains. We let the fresh air brace us, worked our legs against the grade, stomped in the dust, and breathed the scent of sage. Now I sit at my desk with a mug of tea. Phiz sleeps on his bed at my feet, snoring doggie snores. Socrates works at his computer. We have each other. If I suck at a few auditions, it doesn't matter in the grand scheme of things.

CHAPTER 39

STILL HOPING

I went to a movie the other day. I turned off my phone in the theater, which I don't like to do because I don't want to miss a call for an audition. But I reminded myself it's pilot season, and so far this pilot season has been like any other for me, with a quiet phone and plenty of free time.

For two hours I watched famous actors do on the big screen what I've done many times on stage or in "copy-credit-meals" films. The difference between you and me and the stars, besides the size of our salaries, is how we earn them: they get paid to play the juicy parts. We get paid to say, "Here's your coffee, mister."

While the opening credits ran I decided to send a psychic message to my phone so that when I turned it on again there would be a voice-mail from my agent, Blanche, with an audition for a role in a major motion picture. I don't believe in psychic messages, so imagine my shock when lo and behold, after the movie the message was there: an audition for the sequel to a recent blockbuster, to play the wife of the star.

I'm gonna send psychic messages more often.

All the next day I waited for the sides. Finally Blanche's email came. I clicked the attachment and there it was, a page from the script of a huge motion picture. I scrolled down and found my character.

She had one line.

A blasé, not exactly pivotal line. I believe it was, "See you later, honey."

Surely they're not going to cast this important role based on a throw-away line? I thought. I clicked back and read Blanche's email. A one-line part, it said.

My heart felt like someone had blown it up too big then punched it to let the air out. Is this what I came to L.A. for? No. But it's what I've got.

I'm always telling other people to keep their chin up. I say "work hard, do your homework, don't give up." But sometimes that's bullshit. It doesn't always make a difference. I felt sorry for myself.

I'm on my umpteenth year of pounding the Los Angeles pavement. I'm told I'm one of the lucky ones because I work from time to time. Most days I feel that way. Hell, unless you're young and gorgeous you don't just walk onto the set of a major motion picture without experience, even for just one line.

And I had to admit I wanted the part. I looked at the script again. I could do something with "See you later, honey."

I downloaded last summer's prequel and watched it. Okay, I fast-forwarded through the action sequences, but I watched the acting, the romantic stuff and the credits.

I memorized my line.

I chose my outfit, planned my route, got to the audition early, remained calm, maintained a positive attitude, treated everyone professionally, did a good job, enjoyed myself, thanked the casting director and left, feeling good about it.

The next step is to let it go, which I'll do when I finish writing this.

I'm glad for the opportunity to be paid to act, even if it's the tiniest part. Still, I hope for more.

Nobody ever said, "I'm gonna go to Hollywood and become a Bit Player!" It's okay to admit I'd like to be a star. But reality TV has stars. I'm talking about more. I'm talking about that plum, three-dimensional role where I get to lead my character through an emotional life, take the audience with me and get paid for it. It's what I've hoped to be famous for.

Like every young actor, I set out to be more than a journeyman. I wanted to be a great actor. I'm not a young actor anymore. I'm an older, more nuanced actor, and I still hope for a chance to show it. I suppose we all do, or we'd give up.

Actors do give up when they get older. They say, "It's too late, it's not going to happen for me." Perhaps I should get a clue. But I haven't given up yet.

Maybe I'll get the one-line part and it'll be my big break. Maybe it'll be just another job, a paycheck. Or maybe I won't get it. Right now, I need to move on.

Mostly I leave my phone on, but from time to time I turn it off and send it psychic messages, still hoping.

CHAPTER 40
INTERESTING LIVES, PART ONE

Franco Zeffirelli's splendid film of Shakespeare's *Romeo & Juliet*, released in 1968, inspired me to become an actor. The film played for more than a month in my Illinois hometown, and each week I showed up at the theater and watched it over and over until my allowance ran out.

Juliet died young but she had her Romeo, and their short lives were nothing if not interesting. Olivia Hussey portrayed Juliet, and as a bonus she got to speak Shakespeare's language, wear lavish costumes and look heartbreakingly beautiful in glorious settings.

It was settled: I would go to England and become Olivia Hussey as soon as I got my driver's license.

Time melts like a candle, and before I knew it I was ready for college. With no funds for the lure of London, I settled for the University of Illinois. Among other things, I studied Shakespeare. After graduation I moved to Chicago and started trying to make a living as an actor, eventually continuing in Los Angeles.

I got some auditions and some jobs. I got to wear a few fun costumes here and there. I sent out résumés, plugged away, cared less, lost interest. After years in the business I still wasn't making a living, and I forgot what I'd come for. Not only was I not Olivia Hussey, but I had grown too old to play Juliet, and Romeo was nowhere to be found.

If you don't keep your eye on that candle you don't notice how quickly it's melted half away.

One winter's night I went to the movies and saw John Madden's delightful *Shakespeare in Love*. Thirty years had passed since Zeffirelli, but all my youthful excitement came rushing back. It's profound what a writer, an actor and a story can do. As Violet, Gwyneth Paltrow got to speak Shakespeare's language (and, as a bonus, Tom Stoppard's) plus she scored the lavish costumes and glorious settings. On top of that, she looked heartbreakingly beautiful.

It was settled: I had to get to England as soon as possible. I would stand on Shakespeare's own ground and speak his words. I'd wear lavish costumes in glorious settings, and dammit, I'd look beautiful doing it. I already had my driver's license so there were no more excuses.

If you're not a British citizen you can't just show up in England and legally get work, so I figured the best chance I'd have of performing Shakespeare there was an acting class. I decided to audition for the British/American Drama Academy's (BADA's) "Summer at Oxford" because they offered a professional program with teachers I admired. I hired a coach, worked hard on my audition, and got accepted.

When I decided to go the world supported me. I spent the next few months hoarding every penny and working extra shifts at my day job. At birthday time I begged my friends to give me the $3.99 instead of buying a card. They came through, chipping in with not just $3.99 but $10, $20, even $50 birthday gifts toward my trip. My sister and mother gave me cash. My brother gave me his frequent flyer miles. It was thrilling. I ate adrenaline for lunch, which was good because it helped me save on groceries.

Adding to the anticipation was the prediction, from so many friends that I lost count, that I would meet Mr. Right in England. I'm not psychic but my friends were practically having visions. My mother was so afraid it would happen that she insisted I must not get married overseas.

I didn't tell her that if I met the man of my dreams in England, I'd be staying there.

When we students arrived at Oxford our teachers, some of them members of the Royal Shakespeare Company, auditioned us again to place us according to our abilities. They offered different levels, including a class for professionals. I was glad I'd hired a coach. BADA is mostly not folks in their forties but kids fresh out of college and looking for the next Something-To-Do. After 20 years in the business it was a matter of pride for me to get into that professional class. The pro class had the top teachers.

That's how I found myself in a master class, standing in a basement room at Oxford's medieval Balliol College one hot July night. I was shaking, not with fear but with a little bit of agony and a lot of ecstasy, and speaking Sonnet 152 to the legendary John Barton, co-founder (with Sir Peter Hall) of the Royal Shakespeare Company.

The rust-colored carpet and plastic chairs provided a glorious setting. My summer dress was lavish costume enough.

My candle still had plenty of burning to do, and I didn't have to say I never got around to fulfilling a dream. To speak Shakespeare's words, right there on his stompin' grounds, was enough heartbreaking beauty for me.

◆

CHAPTER 41

INTERESTING LIVES, PART TWO

There's a photo of me taken at LAX on my way to England for my adventure at the British/American Drama Academy. I'm standing next to my suitcase wearing sunglasses, dressed in sleek black, a bemused smile on my face. I look calm and poised, even powerful. But inside I was all anticipation and fear. And, I realize now, sadness.

I hoped to find in England something magical, a key to the fulfilling life I hadn't been able to create on my own. I didn't know what the key would be. My friends predicted it would be Mr. Right. That would be nice, but better yet, I wanted a new direction in my career. If I liked England I'd look for a way to stay there and work as an actor. There'd be a sign. I'd watch for it.

The BADA program left little time for seeking signs. It was a four-week intensive with British and American professionals teaching mostly American students. Mornings were filled with voice and movement classes, audition workshops and Shakespeare study, guided by members of the Royal Shakespeare Company. Each week, our afternoons were led by different master teachers, and once a week we had an evening with *their* master, the legendary John Barton, co-founder and associate director of the Royal Shakespeare Company.

I threw myself in, opening to every experience I encountered and every person I met. I was loathe to waste a moment of precious England time. Ever aware of my inner candle, I burned the poor thing at both ends.

For four weeks, five days a week, we had classes all day and sometimes in the evenings, not to mention homework and private tutorials. I attended plays, hung out with my classmates and learned my way around Oxford and the surrounding countryside. Mr. Right was nowhere to be found, but it mattered little. There was history to be absorbed! Castles to be ogled! Ale to be sampled!

By the third week half the people in my class, including me, had colds. The master teacher for that week's afternoon intensives was the great Irish actress, Fiona Shaw. She'd recently garnered raves for her performance in the film *The Butcher Boy*. I'd heard of her stagecraft, too: she'd played most of the great roles for women and, famously, some of the men's. (Harry Potter's Aunt Petunia may help one picture her as Medea, but perhaps not as Richard II.) This was before her American film and TV fame, though I was already in awe of her work.

I adored all of my teachers at BADA. Each was generous and brilliant in their way. Some got to know us as individuals, some were loving and supportive, even cuddly. That wasn't Fiona's style. She didn't get personal. She was intensely interested in us not as individuals, but in what we produced as performers. Each day she arrived ready to work, wearing baggy capris and no make-up, her short-cropped hair brushed out of her face.

I kept a journal at Oxford. Here's my first entry about Fiona Shaw: "I like Fiona; I appreciate that she's prepared to impart knowledge. It would be easy to play on one's fame. But she has a deep interest in the work."

During her week as our master teacher, Fiona helped us free ourselves to explore text in our imaginations. Her tool for this was Samuel Beckett, whose works she loved, even though one of her productions of Beckett had been famously closed down by his estate when she and her director experimented with stage directions in a West End production of *Footfalls*.

Mid-week, my exhausted classmates and I presented our homework. Fiona encouraged us to ignore stage directions and let the text carry us beyond our limits. Despite the coughing and nose-blowing, we threw ourselves into the work. With our bodies, voices and minds we transformed the classroom into a moon, a library, a graveyard. My partner and I waltzed in our penthouse. Another pair read books from each others' backs. Two more performed a striptease that astonished them as much as it did the rest of us.

Fiona would shake her head, wide-eyed. "Extraordinary!" was the word she used when the work pleased her. She said each script is different every time it's performed because the play happens not on the page, but between the actors and each individual member of the audience. She spoke of bringing our best selves to the text, because we light it up with our own experience.

That point was important, she said, because to be good

artists, "we *must* lead interesting lives."

I heard that phrase with my gut.

Tears poured from my eyes before I knew they were coming. Everyone noticed including Fiona, but nobody said anything. Class went on without me while I sat in the back and wondered why I couldn't stop crying.

But I knew the answer. It was because I wasn't Olivia Hussey after all. I was a 43-year-old actress who had never completely made a living in my chosen field. The BADA course was, in many ways, a re-hash of things I already knew. It was a delight to re-learn them, an idyll of art, a reminder of why I was an actor. But in ten days it would be over and I'd have to face reality. I couldn't stay in England legally and work. I hadn't found Mr. Right, nor had I found the magic key that would make my life fulfilling. What would I do at the end of class? How could I return to Los Angeles to my day job and to life as it had been before, after all this joy?

I knew only that I couldn't continue to be what I had been up until the day I'd had my picture taken at LAX. I could no longer pretend to be brave, nor could I pretend my life was okay.

For years I had tried to get work as an actor in Los Angeles. I had concentrated all my efforts on the commercial aspects of the business. I had pandered to the money to the point of forgetting I was an artist. It was breaking my heart.

CHAPTER 42

INTERESTING LIVES, PART THREE

After four weeks at Oxford I wanted to live there—get a job, pay taxes, be an American expat grown-up living in England. But that's not easy to do unless you meet Mr. Right and marry him before your visa runs out. After BADA I spent a couple of blissful weeks in and around London, exploring history and seeing plays. I was mindful of my candle, not willing to waste a moment of a once-in-a-lifetime trip. But soon I was at the end of my money, and going back to L.A. was my only option whether I liked it or not.

It wasn't until after I returned that I began to notice the changes. If you're an unhappy person, you'll be unhappy no matter where you are. The reverse is also true. I had thought going to England would make me happy and it did, but I didn't have to be there to feel the effects. And it wasn't just the going that made me happy. It was being brave enough to go.

I was no longer ruled by fear. I surprised myself. Little

things that had once intimidated me, like auditioning or even just stating a controversial opinion, were now as easy as kicking through a pile of autumn leaves. Speaking of which, I started having more fun and stopped taking myself so seriously.

Bigger changes occurred, too. I discovered that although some people swear acting is everything it's not, at least not for me. I lowered it on my priority list and put happiness higher. There are a thousand other enriching things to do.

I no longer cared to take just any old acting job. I began to say "no" to undignified roles, one-liners or parts that were just plain boring. Yet even though I turned down work, within months I left my day job because I was finally making my living as an actor, doing voice work. And soon I began seeing the man I eventually married, which was lucky because otherwise I might have had to marry myself.

I don't think these changes happened solely because I went to England or studied Shakespeare or cried in Fiona Shaw's class, though those things helped. But I brought my burning candle home with me. (We're speaking figuratively here; don't try to take fire on a plane.) I had thrown myself into my work at Oxford because I knew my time was limited. I still know that. I still do that. Maybe my visit to England was a once-in-a-lifetime trip but hey, life is a once-in-a-lifetime trip. I try to keep that in mind.

I made the decision to go, then I made it happen. It seemed impossible but I did it. Whenever I come up against something difficult I try to remember the power in that. That power is mine.

So in a way, I did meet Mr. Right in England. It's just that he turned out to be me.

• • •

There's a coda to this long-winded story. Some years later I had a few lines in a feature called "Fracture," starring Anthony Hopkins and Ryan Gosling. I appeared in a courtroom scene with the stars.

When I arrived at the shoot I wasn't particularly nervous until I peeked onto the set and saw who was playing the judge: Fiona Shaw. My heart just about flew out of the nicely-pressed blouse the wardrobe ladies had picked out for me. I was going to work with Fiona Shaw!

She didn't recognize me and I didn't expect her to. After we rehearsed the scene she disappeared, so I located the assistant director and told him I had to speak with Ms. Shaw. He pointed to the make-up trailer. It was my chance.

I found her in the trailer with the hair lady. Fiona's once short-cropped, copper hair had grown long and flowing, and while Hair-Lady coiffed and sprayed, I introduced myself to Fiona. She glanced at me in the mirror and didn't discourage me from continuing, so I refreshed her memory with something like "I just want to say hi, I was in your class at BADA in 1999, and it was a great class, and you said something one day that made me cry…"

Her Irish lilt: "Oh? What did I say?"

"You said, 'We *must* lead interesting lives.'"

She looked at me again. "I do remember you."

She did. Recognition lit her eyes and she smiled, then lilted some more. "I take it your life wasn't very interesting 'til then."

"No. It wasn't."

"And has it been more interesting since?"

I nodded and smiled. "Yes. Yes it has."

* * *

We don't get everything we dream of in life. I dreamed of playing Juliet, now I know I never will. This is because dreams aren't actions.

But there are other splendid roles, England is still there, and sometimes we receive gifts we never dreamt of. If you'll forgive the metaphor once more, though my candle has burned down a bit I've still got plenty of wax left to go, and I don't intend to waste a drop of it.

CHAPTER 43
YES/AND

My first professional acting job was with The Second City in Chicago, where the focus was improvisational comedy. We performed without a script which, dichotomously, requires working at the top of your intelligence without thinking too much.

The first rule of improv is "No Denial," otherwise known as "Yes/And." *Yes*, I agree with the other actor's reality, *And* I move the scene forward to the funny bits.

It's not a bad rule for the day-to-day. *Yes*, this is my reality, *And* here's what I'm doing to move forward. It keeps me out of denial and helps me put the funny bits into perspective.

When my first *Act As If* column appeared in NowCasting's *ActorsInk*, my plan was to share the funny bits I'd experienced over the course of my acting career. If you don't revel in the comedy of being an actor, the tragedy can make you one of those actors who gets drunk on denial and name-drops at parties, which makes you a source of ridicule anyway, so you might as well get to the funny bits right from the top.

But *Act As If* quickly became more than a joke forum for me. For four and a half years, writing about my career was part of a learning experience that brought great change to my life.

I learned that:

I will never know everything, about acting or anything else, so there's no sense worrying about it. I might as well say *Yes* to the reality of my ignorance when I'm clueless, *And* admit I'm a pro when I know what I know.

What I know changes. *Yes*, I might have known it yesterday, *And* that doesn't mean I know it today. Some lessons have to be learned more than once. I'll know it again tomorrow.

I have things to teach, even when I make mistakes—*especially* when I make mistakes. If I'm willing to share them, we all get to laugh and we usually learn something. The bigger the screw-up the better. *Yes*, this approach works well, *And*, fortunately, I have a wealth of errors and bad moves upon which to draw.

When I was young I was dedicated to one thing and one thing only. I was an actor, period. When my acting career wasn't going well my reality was misery. In my denial, I got drunk and name-dropped at parties.

Now I'm more than an actor. I'm a writer, publisher, photographer, wife, friend, dog-lover, hiker and more, though I can't think of anything else at the moment (except, you know, driver, grocery shopper, nose-blower and miscellaneous stuff that makes the list boring and too long). The point is, I have other passions. Diversity makes me a happier person and a better artist. For the times when the world doesn't give a damn about my work (and we all know how often those times can be), other interests come in handy. I have things to care about besides whether or not I get a part or sell a story. And my nose-blowing supplies are useful for when I care too much.

I wrote 100 *Act As If* columns. Doing so was the beginning of my transformation from actor to writer. Who'd a thunk it? Life's reality changes from time to time. I may not know where a new focus will lead me, and not knowing is fertile ground where anything can grow. It's improvisation for life. If you work at the top of your intelligence without thinking too much, and without denying your passion, you always find your way.

Yes. *And...*

ACKNOWLEDGEMENTS

First and foremost, I thank Richard Gilbert-Hill. As editor of *ActorsInk* at NowCasting.com, Richard gave me an outlet, a place to try my ideas and connect with other actors. This book would not exist without him. Thanks also to NowCasting, my writing home for over four years.

My undying gratitude goes to Liz Hanley, Greta Hanley and Bicoastal Talent. Without Liz there would be no Blanche, and without their agency I wouldn't have these stories to tell.

Thanks to all the casting directors who offered opportunities, and to the actors who shared their stories with me. Special thanks to Tara Samuel for her insightful notes.

To my office-mate, Boz (Phiz): I miss you so.

All my love to John Sandel. It's not easy to share a family with an actor, or a writer for that matter. You are my home and my heart.

ABOUT THE AUTHOR

Petrea Burchard's acting career moved her from Chicago to Hollywood via stage, television, film and voice-over. She's known as the first English voice of Ryoko, the sexy space pirate in the animé classic, *Tenchi Muyo!* Currently she's the radio and TV voice of a supermarket chain in Southern California.

Her writing career includes *Act As If*, her humor column at NowCasting.com, about the life of a journeyman actor in Hollywood. Her articles, essays, book reviews and short fiction have appeared online and in print. Her first novel, *Camelot & Vine*, was inspired by a trip to England (see "Interesting Lives," Parts One, Two and Three). *Act As If* is her first book of essays.

Petrea is available for speaking engagements, book groups and readings.

PetreaBurchard.com
Facebook.com/PBAuthor
Twitter.com/PetreaBurchard

www.ingramcontent.com/pod-product-compliance
Lightning Source LLC
Chambersburg PA
CBHW020651300426
44112CB00007B/328